UNIVERSITIES & STUDENTS

a guide to rights, responsibilities & practical remedies

G R EVANS JASWINDER GILL

Routledge
Taylor & Francis Group
LONDON AND NEW YORK

The authors have enjoyed their collaboration and would like to thank each other.

G R Evans would like to thank the officers of the Cambridge Students' Union for many interesting hours of discussions.

Jaswinder Gill is grateful to Hannah Reeves for always being dependable in the preparation of this book. He dedicates the book to his father, Autar Singh Gill, for being the perfect role model.

First published in 2001 by Kogan Page Limited

This edition published in 2013 by Routledge
2 Park Square, Milton Park, Abingdon, Oxon OX14 4RN
711 Third Avenue, New York, NY 10017

Routledge is an imprint of the Taylor & Francis Group, an informa business

British Library Cataloguing in Publication Data

A CIP record for this book is available from the British Library.

ISBN 0 7494 3465 1

Typeset by Kogan Page

Contents

Foreword

The Times Higher Education Supplement is delighted to be associated with this guide to the legal framework that binds student and university.

Most people find their university years among the most memorable and enriching of their lives, but inevitably from time to time things go wrong. In the past, it has not always been clear what students can do, or what institutions should do, when this happens although this is now beginning to change. As the number of people entering higher education continues to grow, and as tuition fees turn students into more demanding consumers, institutions face increasing pressure to improve the way they handle complaints. Many are already responding.

This book offers clear information to students and academics about the options open to them if conflicts arise, including some recent key developments. We hope it will prove to be a useful reference point for both students and institutions, and help clear up some of the misunderstandings that can create tensions between the two.

Auriol Stevens
Editor, The Times Higher Education Supplement

Preface

'All students have a legitimate interest in quality and standards in teaching.[1] They and their parents have increasingly become critical consumers.' 'The way complaints are handled says a good deal about how a university views its students, and its readiness to put right what has gone wrong.' In September 1999 the Education and Employment Minister Baroness Blackstone made these remarks to the annual meeting of the Committee of Vice-Chancellors and Principals. Students are now visible, and that makes them politically important; it gives them, as a group, an influence they have not had before. Yet individually they remain as vulnerable as ever to confusion on the part of the 'providers', to poor teaching and incompetent administration.

This book is chiefly about the vulnerabilities of the ordinary student. It is the first extended study to approach the problems from a student's-eye view, incorporating recent developments in the area of 'student matters'.

Far more students are now entering higher education and this rapid expansion, coupled with the transformation of the former polytechnics into universities in 1992, has placed great strains upon the system. This is making it necessary to clarify much that has previously been obscure about the position of students. It is also generating dissatisfactions and complaints, which students are becoming increasingly ready to voice. So student articulation of their perceptions of what is wrong forms an important substrate of any such study. We have done our best to listen to what students are saying.

Universities have been slow off the mark in responding to this culture change. They remain autonomous. They have not had to answer to anyone

1 Both in universities and in courses franchised by universities to be provided by colleges and institutes of higher education.

for what they do until the relatively recent introduction of 'quality assessment' and the principle that funding can be withheld from the 'old' universities if standards are not maintained. The student who feels that he or she has not really been listened to when asking awkward questions may well be right. It is not healthy to allow organizations to police themselves yet if universities do not learn to do so openly, honesty and quickly, there is a danger that they will increasingly be policed by the state, which will bring with it other dangers.

It is better for disputes to be prevented or resolved informally than for them to go through the courts. It is expensive to do things that way and it is slow and uncertain; a student may lose years in battle with his or her university; the university suffers too, both financially and in its reputation.

The best way forward for the student and the university alike is for everyone to understand the ground rules. Students in particular need a practical guide to consult when things go wrong in their time at university because they do not have such ready access to the legal advice that universities can afford. We have taken a student's-eye look at a series of familiar problem areas. The main purpose is to provide students with information about their position in relation to their institution, their rights and the remedies that may be available to them if things go wrong. Those running institutions will also, we hope, find this book useful.

David Lepper MP wrote the following in a letter to the Quality Assurance Agency dated 1 June 1999:

> The general concern which I have picked up is that the world of higher education is one in which generally there is a suspicion that old boy and girl networks dominate and that, particularly in the area of appeals relating to academic awards, there is a difficulty in judging the independence of those involved in administering and operating such procedures.
>
> It is right that a deadline should be set for institutions to be able to demonstrate that they are adhering to precepts contained in the code but there is no indication of what will be the consequences for those institutions which are shown to be failing in this respect.

Abbreviations

CVCP – Committee of Vice-Chancellors and Principals

DfEE – Department for Education and Employment

HC Deb – House of Commons Debates

HL Deb – House of Lords Debates

Hyams – Hyams, O (1998) *Law of Education*, Sweet and Maxwell, London

LEA – Local Education Authority

LQR – *Law Quarterly Review*

PL – *Public Law*

QAA – Quality Assurance Agency

RAE – Research Assessment Exercise

THES – *The Times Higher Education Supplement*

Introduction

Is a university a business? If so, it goes about its trading in a funny way. How many car dealers refuse to sell a car to cash buyers because they do not have the right qualifications? Universities, however, will not admit you to 'buy' their courses unless you do. How many supermarkets refuse to hand over the goods at the cash desk because on the way through the supermarket the shopper did not stop at the bacon counter?[1] If students are late with an assignment or refuse to pay their fees, however, they may be barred from getting their degrees. The student is, in effect, expected to 'pay now and complain later', and even if he or she makes good his or her complaint, it may not be possible for the injustice to be put right. In a commercial and competitive market place that is not in line with recognized consumer rights involving purchase and sale.

Universities are now increasingly seen to have a duty to give value for money in return for public funds. But perhaps the most important change directly affecting students has been the reintroduction of the requirement that students should pay tuition fees. This is the most recent stage in a long development that has fundamentally changed the relationship of students to institutions of higher education. It heightens the presumption that there is a contract. And if there is a contract, the obligations are mutual. The student has to do the work, attend the lectures and seminars, and so on, and pass the examinations for a degree, but he or she is entitled to good quality teaching, adequate facilities and a well-designed course.

Alongside the figure of the student as 'consumer' stands the student as 'stakeholder'. He or she is not the only stakeholder. The government, employers, unions, schools, parents, taxpayers, are stakeholders, too.[2]

1 Adapted from examples in Birtwhistle, T (1998) Student academic appeals: a holistic assessment, *Education and the Law*, **10**, pp 41–54 at p 50.

2 Birtwhistle, T (1998) Student academic appeals: a holistic assessment, *Education and the Law*, **10**, pp 41–54 at pp 48–49.

So the questions 'what is a university?' and 'what is a student?' now have to be answered in new ways that reflect these changing aspects of the relationship between the student and the university.

What is a university?

In the United Kingdom a university normally has powers to award both 'taught' and 'research' degrees; the list now consists of over a hundred institutions. They did not all come into existence in the same way. Oxford and Cambridge have origins so many centuries old that their constitutions have evolved, layer upon layer, into a considerable complexity. Then there is a category of 'old' universities, mostly founded about a hundred years ago; another group of 'old' universities born in the 1960s wave of expansion; a group of the former polytechnics which became universities in 1992; and a few that have been seeking recognition as universities since then.[3]

More important, perhaps, there have been profound changes of concept about what a university is *for*. Even among degrees about whose official authenticity there is no doubt, a degree is worth only what it is perceived to tell the world about the quality of its holder's knowledge or skills. So universities are now beginning to be thought of as 'quality service providers'. This kind of thinking takes students to be 'customers' for, or 'purchasers' of, or 'consumers' of what is being 'provided'. That fits with the idea that their teachers are professionals who have the same duty to maintain high professional standards as those in other professions. All sorts of obligations follow from that.

But there are other ways of approaching the problem of the need to make sure that students get a good education. Universities used to think of themselves as 'communities of scholarship'. Students and staff were first and foremost 'members' of the university – as in many places they still are.[4] The pattern derived from the mediaeval *universitas*, which was a guild (rather like a cross between a modern professional association and a

---

3 There is a convenient summary of the different types of university in Hyams, O (1998) *Law of Education*, Sweet & Maxwell, London, p 497.

4 See pp 37–38.

modern 'trade union'). The students were the equivalent of apprentices; the Bachelors of Arts were like the journeymen and the Masters of the gild (Masters of Arts) were the teachers who formed the corporate body. The university set its own standards and answered to itself. It ran a closed shop, but it also determined for itself the nature and purpose of the work carried out within it, what 'intellectual skills' and what 'knowledge' it valued, and would reward both teachers and taught. There were advantages to the old model. It was humane and flexible and it encouraged the independence of mind that has made universities able to offer a public service in resisting the pressures of the state to conform to the changing political agenda.

The attitudes this bred have proved extremely persistent in upholding the ideal of university autonomy. Autonomy is a good thing in that it discourages interference by the state with the conduct of universities' legitimate academic business. It is less clearly a good thing if it makes it difficult to call universities to account if they do not maintain standards, do the right thing by their students and staff, and fulfil their traditional purposes of fostering education, learning and research. The point of balance between these two priorities is crucial now.

Governments have stood back from interfering directly in the way universities conduct their affairs, but this traditional autonomy remains a true independence only as long as it is coupled with financial independence – and universities are becoming less financially independent. A university may *govern* itself, but the state increasingly interferes with its running by the simple pragmatic method of giving or withholding funding on condition of compliance with government wishes ('conditions of grant'). Most higher education institutions (the private University of Buckingham is one exception) are funded by the Higher Education Funding Councils,[5] which can require the repayment in whole or in part of the sums so paid.[6] There are further statutory powers. A Higher Education Funding Council 'may arrange for the promotion or carrying out by any person of studies designed to improve economy, efficiency and effectiveness in the management or operations of an institution within the higher education sector'.[7] It

5 The Further and Higher Education Act 1992, s65, provides that HEFC shall fund activities carried on by 'higher education institutions', that is the 'provision of education' and the 'undertaking of research'.

6 Hyams, O (1998) *Law of Education,* Sweet & Maxwell, London, p 502.

7 The Further and Higher Education Act 1992, s83(1).

may require the governing body of any institution within the higher education sector 'to give information to the Council'.[8] The Secretary of State has powers to give directions[9] and even to dissolve a higher education corporation.[10] So the potential for state interference is quite considerable.

The effect on students

The implications of these shifts for students are only gradually becoming clear. On the one hand there is a clear advantage in being a 'customer', because customers can complain about shoddy or unsatisfactory goods or service. This, however, is not an arena in which student customers, or consumers, are the most powerful voice. They are unequal in their bargaining power not only with the universities but also with 'funders' who may have their own agendas. Commercial funders are becoming increasingly necessary to cash-strapped institutions, which are not being fully or adequately funded by the state, and where their money is needed they may be able to call some of the tunes. The commercial funders may want pieces of scientific research and development done, and for that purpose they may wish to arrange for the time of leading scientists, who would otherwise be joining in the teaching of students, to be given to their own projects. The government, too, has been allocating funding on the basis of the outcomes of the Research Assessment Exercises, and that has led to a scramble for research-active academic staff and to complaints that good teaching is devalued in universities' structures of reward.

The introduction of business methods and business ethics may lead to greater efficiency, but that will probably mean that efficiency will be defined in terms of measurable outcomes. There is a visible loss of the old comfortable stretchiness in the system, of room for leisurely growth and sheer 'conversation' with tutors and supervisors and lecturers.

There have also been well-authenticated instances of 'dumbing down', where pressure has been put on teachers to pass more students or to diminish the content or lower the standards of courses. For example, one student

8 The Further and Higher Education Act 1992, s79.
9 The Further and Higher Education Act 1992, s81(1) and 89.
10 The Further and Higher Education Act 1992, s121.

who returned to higher education at the age of 34, chose the course in product design and manufacture for a BEng(Hons) degree at a local college because it was geographically convenient for him to study there and he saw that the degree offered was from an 'old' university. He was also assured when he went to the college for an interview that the course was 'properly validated and accredited by the Institute of Mechanical Engineering'. He originally enrolled for the BSc (Hons) in computer aided design and manufacture, intending to transfer to the product design and manufacture course if he found that he could cope with the mathematics required. He made the transfer with four others at the beginning of the second year. They understood that the course was still validated by the IMechE.

What he found at the local college was a standard that he alleges was so low that, for example, only six or seven out of nearly 40 students on the course had fulfilled the entry requirement of A-level mathematics.

He learned that from October 1997 the university was ceasing to award degrees for the college's courses because, he understood, it was concerned about the standards. A large percentage of students failed the first year of the course. The course leader left the faculty. The number of hours of assisted study fell from 16 to 13 per week (against a norm of over 19 on a government definition of what constituted a full-time course).

He put together a list of complaints, which was signed by a number of students on the course and sent to the Dean of Faculty at the local college. He sent a copy to the university, but received no response. He learned that the IMechE had withdrawn its accreditation from the course.

Pressure was put on the examiners to 'remark papers and pass a much higher number of students'. After more than two years' pressure he began to get acknowledgement that the course had indeed been 'dumbed down', elements had been removed from the course, quantitatively less was being asked and what was required was more elementary.

The question raised by this articulate and persistent mature student was whether the university could be called to account for its failure to police the provision of the course on which its own degrees were being awarded by the college. 'What I have witnessed is...the failure of...the systems put in place to police higher education,' he writes.

That is a natural reaction to the sense of helplessness many students feel in the face of what seems a failure to provide what they have been promised. The problem is that government intervention would not necessarily make things better or be primarily motivated by the wish to improve standards as an end in itself. The question of how universities are to be brought up to standard in their *treatment* of students (a matter inseparable from the maintenance of academic standards) without losing their academic autonomy will hover throughout the text of this book.

What, in such changing times, is a student? Or, perhaps most importantly in the new emerging framework, 'the ordinary student'? One answer can still be given in terms of the idea that a student is there to *study* something, that is, to learn and receive a qualification. From the university's point of view the student is also a source of money, or prestige, if he or she is a very able student. The old idea of the student as a child, *in statu pupillari*, continues to be important in the sense that staff and student are inevitably unequal in any confrontation. Yet modern management talk of 'partnership' and 'stakeholding' ought to be incompatible with such inequality. The student of university age is now (usually) legally an adult and that makes a difference; he is a citizen, a consumer like any other 'purchaser' of a 'service' or a 'product'.

For individual students now, and for universities anxious to get it right, the way forward is through the examination of individual cases and the patterns which emerge from them. We have used them in this book as a way of shaping the discussion.

There is inevitably a good deal here that assumes a basis of legal knowledge, but we hope that students will still find this book user-friendly. The 'student action checklists' are included as a starting point for students whose first need is to know 'what to do' and 'what to look out for'. These feature at the end of each chapter.

1

Becoming a student

The prospectus: reading between the lines

> We hope this Prospectus will enable you to get a clear picture of what we have to offer and that you will find something in it which corresponds to your own aspirations.[1]

> Our aim is to provide the best possible range of Higher Education study opportunities.[2]

These are examples of the ways in which universities now tend to offer their wares. The way they present themselves may tell you a good deal about the kind of place a university is. What does it 'sell' as its advantages?

The prospectus, which sets out what the university is offering and describes the facilities and the courses on offer, may have as much to say about the scenery as about the university. Portsmouth's Undergraduate Prospectus in 1998 said:

> The student experience is so much more than lectures, libraries and laboratories...Portsmouth has something special for all tastes and ages. We welcome you to experience Portsmouth's rich maritime and historical heritage, its unspoilt coastline for water sports or leisurely enjoyment, its busy and varied shopping centre or its lively social scene in pubs, clubs and

1 Undergraduate Prospectus, Newcastle, 1997.
2 Undergraduate Prospectus, Newcastle, 1997.

> restaurants…Portsmouth provides the ideal place to study for your degree and enjoy yourself.

It can be bland and vague:

> The University is committed to achieving excellence in teaching and research. We monitor all our programmes constantly to maintain a learning environment of the highest quality.[3]

You may notice things which are not being said:

> All new lecturing staff undertake a Certificate in Learning and Teaching in Higher Education during their period of probation to promote good practice.[4]

But most lecturers in the old universities have been in post for a long time and will not be caught by this provision, or by any training requirement.

> The University has in place strict procedures for assuring and enhancing the quality of its provision.[5]

But the reader is not told where these may be found. The student is promised:

> a personal tutor/supervisor who is responsible for your academic progress and can guide you towards the appropriate University service for any non-academic queries.[6]

But those services may be far from all embracing, especially when it comes to raising complaints or concerns.

Additional, more detailed, information about particular courses may also be sent out to inquirers. The prospectus is the main selling tool in that it enables the university to 'market' courses, which it offers to prospective students. The promotional literature may be glossy and enticing, designed to induce students to choose the university's courses and to part with their

---

3 Undergraduate Prospectus, Newcastle, 1997.
4 Undergraduate Prospectus, Newcastle, 1997.
5 Undergraduate Prospectus, Newcastle, 1997.
6 Undergraduate Prospectus, Newcastle, 1997.

money. This is now quite consciously a process of marketing. *Education Marketing* is published by Heist, Marketing Services for University and Colleges, with such headings as: 'Maximizing your marketing potential'; 'Marketing marketing'; 'Opinion-brand value' (Issue 13, March 1998). There are also (increasingly) promises made in material on the Internet, the newest 'selling tool' to be used to market the 'wares' of universities. The Internet reaches the international market directly and gives the university a global market place.

All of these publications are like holiday brochures in the sense that they make promises that bind the university, and that is the important point to keep in view. A couple was awarded damages in 1999 because photographs taken at their wedding abroad were of poor quality and so the holiday company's promise of a 'dream holiday' was broken (*The Times,* 1 September 1999). The point that mattered was that this was a very important occasion for the couple. The courts may award damages for broken promises in prospectuses in a similar way, and universities should bear that in mind in 'marketing'. A degree course is very important to the student; it is a big investment carrying all sorts of consequences for the student's professional future or career. One student was awarded £10,000 for a ruined graduation ceremony.

So prospective students should read any literature carefully and make note of any oral promises made on a visit or at an interview that seem to go beyond what is in print, or to conflict with it. That may be important if there is any disagreement later about what was in the stated ('express') or understood ('implied') terms of the contract between the student and the university.

Student charters

Students are now increasingly regarded as customers or clients, to whom the university is providing a service, so many universities have begun to produce 'student charters' on the model of the government's citizen's 'charters', which make promises. These are a recognition that along with the idea of 'student as customer' goes the principle that 'purchasers' have rights to get what they are paying for or to be compensated if they do not. These too are documents that become part of the university's bargain with the student.[7] They may tell the student important things about the attitude of the university towards its students.

A good 'student charter' is clear, accessible, easy to read and sets out some of the key terms of a mutual 'deal' between the university and the student. It is important that the university recognize this mutuality, because it encourages the university to treat the student with respect and dignity. But there is a legal edge to it too because all contracts are two-sided, and this 'deal' is really a contract.

The rights of students who rely on the university's promises

The institution is bound by its promises in the prospectus and charter and any other documents of that sort if the student accepts an offer on the understanding that what he or she has been told is true. The university is bound by what it has said not just because it has published this information but because the student has relied on it, and has entered into an agreement on the basis of it.[8]

The university is bound not only by the 'express' terms in which it made the offer, but also by the implicit terms that can reasonably be taken to be understood. It is also bound by promises made orally. Here the university can be sued for 'misrepresentation' just as much as if it had made a promise in a glossy brochure. A misrepresentation occurs when someone makes an untrue statement of fact during the course of negotiations, which induces the person to whom it is made to enter into a contract with the maker of the statement. For example, if the course leader at the interview provides details of the course and the facilities, it is reasonable for the interviewee to expect the university to be bound by such promises. That is particularly relevant where the student relied on the promises and chose the course accordingly, and then paid the fees for it. It is even more important when as a result of believing such promises the student has suffered detriment. (For example because the course did not, in the end, contain elements it said it would contain, which were especially important to the student's future plans.)

---

7 The Citizen's Charter is a model for this.

8 *D'Mello v Loughborough College of Technology* (1970) 114 SJ 665.

Often a university or college will include a statement or 'disclaimer clause' in its prospectus to say that it is not bound by what the prospectus contains, and that may mean that it can escape liability. Or the university may put in a clause saying that it reserves the right to make changes in the courses. Clauses must satisfy the test of reasonableness or they can be declared void. The Unfair Terms in Consumer Contracts Regulations 1994 and 1999 outlaw anything that makes those who enter into a contract more unequal than they need be.[9] A student 'contracting' with a university for a course is in a very weak position relative to the university that is offering it.

An overseas student who applied to a London University institution to do a postgraduate degree was given a copy of the standard terms applicable to the course, which said that the fees were the same for all students and payable in advance, with appropriate rates for part-time study. The student began the course. She was not satisfied with one of the three taught elements and it was agreed that she should become a part-time student and take a different third course in her second year, when she would also do her dissertation. She then received an additional bill for the third course, calculated on a part-time basis. She was dismayed, because she believed that she had already paid for a 'third course' in her first year's full-time fee, that the institution had accepted that the course she had taken was sub-standard and the new course was simply a replacement of these 'shoddy goods'. She complained, but heard nothing.

Meanwhile she completed her first year and passed her examinations. There was a lengthy dispute about the fees that she should pay. In the end the student agreed to borrow £1,200 from the institution and she signed an agreement in which she accepted that if any tuition fees were outstanding when she finished her course the degree results would be withheld until she had cleared the debt. She claimed that she was pressurized into accepting this loan agreement by being excluded from classes and refused access to the library.

This was arguably a situation in which the new 'contract terms' were unfair. The student was left with little choice but to sign the loan agreement

---

9 Any term that, contrary to the requirement of good faith, causes a significant imbalance in the parties' rights and obligations under the contract to the detriment of the consumer. See the Unfair Contract Terms Act 1977 and the Unfair Terms in Consumer Contracts Regulations 1994 Statutory Instruments 1994, N.3159, Regulation 3(1).

if she wanted to continue with her studies and the institution was able to force her to waive any rights she had to the award of her degree until she had fulfilled this unfair contract term. The bargaining positions of the parties were clearly unequal.

That sort of imbalance would, for example, be created by an agreement binding on the consumer, where the provider can choose whether or not to fulfil it; or irrevocably binding the consumer to terms with which he or she had no real opportunity of becoming acquainted before agreeing to the contract; or 'excluding or hindering the consumer's right to take legal action or exercise any other legal remedy, particularly by requiring the consumer to take disputes exclusively to arbitration not covered by legal provisions'.[10]

These rules are designed to prevent the stronger party from escaping the consequences of not 'delivering' what it has promised. One way in which it can attempt this is to argue that circumstances beyond its control prevented it. An institution may say[11] that it offered the course in good faith but something has happened since that makes it impossible for it to 'deliver' it. For example, there might be special expertise in a particular area in a subject but the member of the academic staff may have moved on to another institution. Or it might become uneconomic to run a given course because not enough students apply for it.[12]

That would be less likely to be accepted if, as a result, a particular student could not then do what he or she had come to the university to do. If a postgraduate were admitted to work with a particular supervisor and the supervisor left the employ of the institution, the university might have a duty to appoint another appropriate supervisor. Or if the institution admits a student to a course it may have to provide that course as it has 'advertised' it. *Cadells v Balfour* in 1980 established that when two medical students had attended a college on the basis of its prospectus, and had paid fees for the course, a contract had been established and the college had an obligation to provide the course.

---

10 Ibid. Schedule 3. See also Hyams, pp 534–36.

11 Under the doctrine of 'supervening impossibility'.

12 *Davis Contractors Ltd v Fareham Urban District Council* [1956] AC 696 at 729, on the 'unexpected event that...changes the face of things'. In that case, 'at some stage before completion the original contract was dissolved because it became incapable of being performed according to its true significance'.

The question that a court would look at here in a particular case would be the balance of convenience. Would it be more damaging to the student not to provide the course than it was inconvenient for the university to have to do what it had promised?[13]

Clare Casson and Amanda O'Brien were admitted to study human communication at the University of Aston in Birmingham, a course listed in the undergraduate prospectus for 1981–82. Both were offered places, which both accepted. The University found that it could not mount the course. Both were then offered places on an alternative course called 'human psychology'. They then tried to sue for breach of contract under the old contract (that is, the contract to 'deliver' the first course). It was held that they had accepted the substitute places and that this 'effectively substituted the new obligations for the old and put an end to the rights of either party under the old contract'. The important question of the rights of those who have not yet been admitted to challenge the decision of a university was not directly addressed here, since both students were admitted (although one had withdrawn at the time of the case).

The Sunday Times of August 1999 carried a report of a group of cases. On 27 May 1999, a student was awarded the remedy of specific performance and was reinstated on her course. Two students claimed loss of earnings for loss of chance and opportunity, because she was unable to make progress in her career as a social worker. The College of Further and Higher Education was held to be in breach of contract.[14] Damages were awarded in the sum of £70,000 for both students and both later qualified. Another student was granted a similar remedy. Yet another was able to obtain an out-of-court settlement because the institution failed to provide the course it had promised.

---

13 Cases on promises in prospectuses:
Casson v University of Aston in Birmingham [1983] 1 All ER 88; *D'Mello v Loughborough College of Technology* (*The Times*, 17 June 1970); *Sammy v Birkbeck College* (*The Times*, 3 November 1964); *Moran v University College, Salford* (1993) (*The Times*, 23 November); *Sammy v Birkbeck College* (1964) (*The Times*, 3 November).

14 Reported in *The Sunday Times*, August 1999, p 13.

Getting a place

Access

In May 2000 a political storm blew up when Magdalen College, Oxford, rejected a candidate for admission to a medical course. The applicant had excellent GCSE grades but she had been to a comprehensive school and the Chancellor of the Exchequer, at a bleak moment in Labour Party fortunes, seized on the chance to call for an end to admissions practices that appeared to make it more difficult for children from state schools to enter university, especially the 'élite' universities at the top of the league-tables. The statistical trend, in fact, showed that this problem was in the process of being solved and the previous year there had even been complaints from public schools that it was not fair to their pupils to be discriminated *against* when they had earned their grades fairly and squarely.

'Access' has become a political 'hot potato', because although universities want to claim that they have the pick of the most able students (for this demonstrates that they are the top universities) they are embarrassed if it turns out that a high proportion of those they take come from public schools, or are white and male. There have been problems – especially for Oxford and Cambridge – in getting proportions of racial minorities and women and disabled students to match those in society at large. Oxford and Cambridge find it difficult to encourage enough applications from state schools because of a perception that so many of their students come from public schools and it would be 'hard to get in'. The problems now are probably mainly of persuading prospective students to apply, rather than of failure on the part of institutions to realize that they have a duty to treat all applicants equally. It is important to solve the 'access' problem if the full range of university options is really to be open to everyone.

The underlying problems are complex. There is the question of persuading applicants from schools without a tradition of sending pupils to university even to try for places, as well as the difficulty of ensuring that they have a fair and equal chance to get in if they do apply. Positive discrimination can diminish the perception of the real achievement of those who are successful.

Admission

Admission to universities has always been in the universities' own hands. This goes back to the ancient principle that they were admitting members to a 'domestic' or 'private' body of scholars, *junior* members certainly, but still people whom they were at liberty to choose not to let in. Things have moved on a good deal because the autonomy of universities is less secure when they depend heavily on public funding, and in May 2000 the government was proposing to use allocation of funding as a reward for universities that admitted a quota of pupils from state schools, and 'punishing' financially those that did not.

The situation is also altered by the increasing importance of the recognition that there is a contract with the student. In *Clark v University of Lincolnshire and Humberside* [2000] CA (*The Times*, 3 May 2000) it was held that the court could adjudicate on an action for breach of contractual rules brought by a student against a higher education corporation or new university that had no provision for the supervisory jurisdiction of a visitor. Sedley LJ, says that 'while capable, like most contractual disputes, of domestic resolution, there are allegations of breach of contract on which the courts are well able to adjudicate'.

So we need to begin by looking at the ground rules of a fair and lawful admissions policy and practice. There should be a clear statement of any matriculation requirements, that is, number or level of passes in GCSE or A Level, whether mature students may have these waived, and in what circumstances. It should be made clear whether the responsibility to ask for exemptions lies with the applicant and what kinds of previous experience or study may be counted towards admission to particular courses.

The decision about acceptance or rejection is still made by the university or college. At Oxford and Cambridge the college decides whom to admit and the student then automatically becomes a student at the university. No outside agency can force anyone to give a student a place. That is because the law treats a university for this purpose as if it were a private club, which has a right to choose whom it will admit.[15] The university has a good deal of freedom to choose as it pleases. For example, because it controls its own admissions, a university can choose whether or not even to interview the

15 *Weinberger and Inglis* [1919] AC 606 at 631, 636, 642. *Nagle v Fielden* [1996] 2 QB 633 at 693.

student, what policies to follow in choosing, or what evidence to take into account in making its decision. The university does not have to give reasons for rejection, so it may be difficult to establish grounds for legitimate complaint.[16]

No one has a 'right' to be admitted. But from an applicant's point of view there is not only the question whether the university is making its decisions efficiently and with clear rules, but also whether it is doing it fairly. A university has a duty to run a fair and open competition for places. Some Oxford and Cambridge colleges have ancient scholarships, which were set up with curious restrictions that give an advantage to particular candidates. It may be very difficult to alter the terms of such a gift to fit modern society. Today admissions tutors have a duty to decide whether to admit candidates, on merit and in a fair competition with others. There have been attempts to guarantee places to those doing access courses at the institution, or to those coming from a particular college or school, or from a particular business or industry. Those may be acceptable arrangements provided they do not give advantage to certain candidates in what is advertised as an open competition on merit.

A story

In this fictitious case, James applies to do physics at Ludlow. He has A levels already (B, D, D) and, while 'having time out', has decided, after all, despite a chequered school career and very weak GCSEs, to enter higher education. He is interviewed by a Dr Sparky, a physics academic, who tells him: 'no problem, you have a place'. His former sixth-form teacher thinks that Ludlow invariably demands B, B, B for physics and phones Dr Sparky to query this 'offer' with the physics academic, who, in irritation, confirms it to the teacher. James turns down the chance to be interviewed at both Ipswich and Scunthorpe, and contentedly awaits the UCAS written confirmation of the offer. He next receives a rejection from Ludlow via UCAS. Anxiously he phones physics at Ludlow and is told by the departmental secretary that the physics academic who interviewed him was only standing in for the departmental admissions tutor, who had been off ill that week,

16 *McInnes v Onslow Fane* [1978] 3 All ER 211 at 222.

and that Dr Sparky (having recently arrived from Ipswich) mistakenly believed that Ludlow also accepted physics students at C, D, D or above.[17]

In this story, the university made a good many mistakes. It allowed someone who had not been properly empowered to do so to give an interviewee information that was, in any case, inaccurate, and a promise that he did not have the authority to make. Those were not things that the interviewee could have known and he could hardly have asked whether the person interviewing him knew what he was doing. And so he made a decision that badly affected his prospects for the future.

Treating applicants equally

A university is not allowed to refuse a place on grounds of *nationality* or *sex,* because that would be racial or sexual discrimination.[18]

The same duty not to discriminate does not yet apply to disabled students, who are not explicitly protected against such discrimination by the Disability Discrimination Act 1995. Consultation is currently taking place with a view to extending the statutory protection, but there is as yet no Bill. Moreover, there are many untested questions about what conditions would amount to a 'disability' and qualify for any legal protection and it may be difficult to show that there has been actual discrimination (in other words, treating someone differently because of a disability) because the university could always argue that there were purely academic grounds for any decision it made about a student.

The university should make *reasonable* provisions in the spirit of the Disability Discrimination Act 1995 to enable disabled students to be admitted and to follow the course as though they were students of similar ability who were not disabled. The rule about 'reasonableness' means, for example, that it might be 'reasonable' to expect the university to put in ramps for wheelchair access, but it would not be 'reasonable' to expect it to move a whole department to another building or pull down an inconvenient 'listed' building. Cambridge's Department of Architecture is in an old

---

17 This fictional example is used with grateful acknowledgement to David Palfreyman, who provided it for an OECD Conference at New College, Oxford, 20–22 September, 1999.

18 Race Relations Act 1976 s17. Sex Discrimination Act 1975 s22.

rambling building that was totally inaccessible to someone in a wheelchair. The academic architects who worked in it did not see how to get round that difficulty for one student who would have been in a wheelchair, but it would not have been reasonable to require the University to build a whole new department. An Oxford college admitted a paraplegic student and adapted a lift so that he could get into the hall for meals, but it could not alter its ancient buildings to give him access to them all, and the law would not require it to do so, but the university could find itself in difficulties if it gave assurances it could not fulfil. For example, if a student in a wheelchair was told that there was disabled access to the library on the campus he would have a reasonable expectation that he would be able to use the library facilities. If he accepted the offer and went to the university on that understanding and then found that there was no disabled access, he would have a case for breach of contract.

Universities usually mean well in their dealings with disabled students but there can be a good deal of ignorance on the part of admissions officers about what is feasible, and a disabled student is likely to have to educate the university in exactly what it means to be him or her, with his disability or combination of disabilities.

A student with lupus, an exhausting autoimmune disease, applied for university entrance. She looked perfectly normal, and it was hard for the admissions tutor to grasp that she would need help in getting about the university because she could not walk long distances and that she would need time to rest in the middle of examinations. She tried unsuccessfully to gain entrance to various colleges, which did not want to take on an 'invalid'. It took an imaginative admissions tutor to say, 'We use taxis to take the rugby team to and from the training ground. I don't see why we shouldn't afford taxis for you sometimes.'

For those students who prefer not to tell the university about their disability and where the disability is not obvious, a balance has to be struck between the right to privacy and the need for the university to be given fair warning of problems. If, for instance, a student failed an examination because he did not explain that he needed extra time, he could not complain later.

Treating applicants fairly

Having a degree will make a great difference to someone's future career. There has been an attempt to argue that a university has a duty to bear in mind the enormous importance to the candidate of gaining a university place. Nevertheless, there are a great many universities, so it could not be held that only the university in question could supply what was needed. That would make it difficult to use this argument to challenge any particular institution that refused admission, unless the course it offered was uniquely suitable so that no other university would do. So for all practical purposes 'gaining a place' is a matter between the particular would-be student and the particular university.

It would be possible to base a complaint upon the standard points that can be used to challenge the conduct of the procedure as 'unfair', for example, that the procedure itself was inherently unfair or that something that ought to have been taken into account was ignored or something was taken into account that ought to have been disregarded.[19]

Interviews

If an interview is held, this in itself creates certain duties. It must be conducted fairly. An admissions tutor at Trinity College, Cambridge, caused great offence in 1998 by allegedly making insulting remarks to an interviewee. That was a publicity disaster for the University, at a time when it was trying to encourage applications from students from backgrounds without a tradition of 'going to Cambridge'.

The college might have found itself in deeper difficulties if the student had tried to go to court about the denial of the right to a fair interview. That has been attempted. In *Reilly v University of Glasgow* [1996] ELR 394 a student had applied to study medicine. He had good A-level grades and he was interviewed. The prospectus said that applicants for the medical course were expected to 'have made some personal effort to acquaint themselves with the way of life a medical career offers, and will have come to a personal decision that they are suited to it'. When Mr Reilly was interviewed he realized that the university had expected him to obtain something like 'work

---

19 See pp 64–66 on this type of challenge.

experience' to prove his commitment. In the reasons for rejecting him he was told 'you had not made any independent effort to acquaint yourself with the way of life a medical career offers. This should have involved work shadowing in a general practice or in a hospital or voluntary work in a caring environment'. In the end, he failed to obtain judicial review[20] of this decision but the challenge might well have succeeded and the case was a salutary reminder to universities of the importance of being clear about what they were doing in conducting admission interviews.

Other aspects of 'doing things fairly' may be relevant – whether the admissions tutors have a list of criteria and whether they apply them consistently, and so on.

Fees and loans

Loans

From 1998–99 a loan scheme[21] has been in place, progressively replacing the *maintenance* grant that used to be available. It depends on parental income. Most undergraduates are entitled to about three-quarters of the maximum loan of £3,725 for students beginning their courses in 2000–01, and the remaining quarter is means tested against the family income. Some means-tested supplementary grants can still be had, for support of dependants and where there are course-related costs arising from a disability. There is the possibility of a £250 additional hardship loan (but still only a loan). One or two gaps have been filled. For instance, it is accepted that students who have been 'in care' should be able to receive a maintenance grant to bridge the gap and cover housing during the long vacation before they go to university.

20 See pp 139–41.

21 Under the Education (Student Loans) Act 1990, which was amended by the Education (Student Loans) Act 1998, and the Education (Student Loans) Regulations 1998 the Secretary of State for Education has powers to make arrangements under which students who are eligible (that is students on specified types of course) may take out loans on special terms to pay for their maintenance at university. Statutory Instruments 1998, nos 211, 1676, 2005.

Fees

University students have also had to pay their own *tuition* fees from the beginning of the 1998–99 academic year.

At the time of writing it is unclear whether Article 2 of the First Protocol of the European Convention of Human Rights will apply. This says that 'no person shall be denied the right to education'. The Protocol is concerned primarily with elementary education but applications about higher education matters have been admitted, for example *X v United Kingdom* (1980) 23 DR 228. The difficulty will be the availability of resources. The Human Rights Act 1998, Schedule 3, Part 2, stipulates that the UK accepts Article 2 'only so far as it is compatible with the provision of efficient instruction and training and the avoidance of unreasonable public expenditure'.

The Times of 7 July 2000 carried an article on the Greenaway Report. This was a report commissioned by the Russell Group,[22] an informal 'group' of some of the top-rated universities, into the possibilities of charging top-up fees – that is, higher fees to go to some universities or to do certain courses. This proposal, whose future is hard to predict at the time of writing, is likely to present additional difficulties to students on low incomes, for it is not clear that the waiving of the flat fee, which was first introduced, would extend to the waiving of a wide range of fees, some enormously greater than others. Will students on low incomes have to choose courses from a 'low-fee-band' university? That might affect access severely and make it extremely difficult to ensure that all students can seek places simply on merit.

At present those whose parents have a low income do not have to pay tuition fees. Some students on some courses have an automatic right to have their fees paid if the family income is too low for it to be reasonable for them to afford it. With the cut-off age for classification as a mature student set at a level where a student may well be already a parent while still being assessed on his or her own parents' income, however, there is room for a good deal of anomaly. Students on benefit have their fees waived from 1999. Students who remain eligible to have their fees paid still face the 'mandatory'/'discretionary' barrier, which divides types of course where

22 www.nottingham.ac.uk/economics/funding.

fees have to be paid by the LEA from those where the LEA has a discretion whether to pay them or not. Most full-time first degree courses at UK universities come into the 'mandatory' category, whereas 'vocational' courses are usually discretionary.[23]

The requirement applies to UK full-time undergraduates and EU full-time undergraduates. Students in Scottish universities do four-year courses and students who are themselves Scottish or from the EU do not pay the fee for the fourth year. At the time of writing, other UK students going to Scottish universities continue to have to pay it, anomalous and unfair though this is.

There is going to be a rising scale. The £1,000 charged in the first year of the new scheme went up, in line with inflation, to £1,025 in the second and £1,050 in 2000–01.

Can the payment of fees be enforced? There were one or two high-profile challenges in the first year, notably from a group of Oxford undergraduates who demonstrated and protested. The *Times Higher Education Supplement* of 30 July 1999 ran a front-page story giving large figures for unpaid debts, with considerable numbers of students at some universities not having paid their fees for the first year. There were suggestions that students might not be registered for their second year or that they might be refused the award of their degrees at the end of their courses if they did not pay.

Universities cannot enforce the repayment of debts unless they can show that they have a legal entitlement to the money and a right to enforce the payment in the way they have chosen.[24] Often universities set out the regulations governing the ways in which they will recover debts in documents that are not made available to the student before he or she accepts the place or registers as a student. If universities make regulations to give themselves powers to withhold examination results or prevent attendance at lectures for non-payment of *non-academic* debts, that might be unenforceable and the courts might disapprove. However, there is likely to be an important difference in the eyes of judges between enforcement of debts for accommodation and enforcement of payment of tuition fees.

---

23 See pp 84–87 on the exercise of discretion.

24 Elaine Maxwell, 'Enforcement – the university as creditor', paper given at RAWS Conference, Sheffield, 24 March 1999.

Students 'on benefit'

The situation of students on benefit can be desperately frustrating. A student whose husband was claiming income support and housing benefit was given a grant for a course. The Department of Social Security told the couple that they must pay back the benefits. The amount, nearly £3,000, was progressively deducted from their income support. For two of the three years of the BSc degree this student was taking she received no grant. She could not pay the fees. She received invoices for the fees, with a sum added for interest. She complained that she had been entitled to a mandatory award and that she had not been told why she had not received it, that the benefits that had been paid in error were being paid back, and the two matters ought to have been treated separately.

This confusion led to a situation where, when her final examination results were ready in 1999 she was refused them, and also her degree, until she had paid the fees.

Students wishing to transfer to another institution

Another group that may encounter special difficulties are the students who want to transfer from one institution to another. One student who needed to do so because she believed that she was not receiving the course she had been promised at the first institution had great difficulty in getting the college to which the transfer was made to write to the local authority by the deadline so that her grant could be transferred.

Part-time students

Part-time students have rights in connection with admission and the provision of the courses they have been accepted for because they, too, have a contract with the institution, but they will normally pay a smaller fee. That makes it important to be clear when a course or a student is 'part time'.

There are difficulties in deciding what constitutes full and what part-time education. In 1996 the DfEE wrote a letter in which it admitted:

> There is no definition of what constitutes full-time education, so institutions must use their own judgement...The judgement is in the end a

> common sense one. A course designed on the basis that it will fill an ordinary working week constitutes full-time education, and one that is designed to allow other activity before an ordinary working week is filled constitutes part-time education. Of course, it is possible to receive full-time education and also work part-time and work full-time and also receive part-time education...a course could constitute part-time education if it is of such a duration that it does not interrupt an ordinary working year. A fortnight's course, while full-time for a fortnight, could properly be regarded as part-time education... A free-standing course that is designed to fill a whole term is almost certainly full-time education during that period. If, on the other hand, it is part of a longer course, in which work and study alternate, it may be that the longer course is properly regarded as a part-time course.[25]

These problems remain unresolved, and this kind of logic chopping can be important in determining whether a student owes the institution the full-time fee. From the autumn of 2000 loans of at least £500 will be available for students on low incomes on part-time courses, to help with their fees.

Overseas students

Overseas students are another category in an anomalous position. Once they are admitted, they have the same contractual rights as other students but they face a hurdle in the calculation of the fees they are due to pay, depending on their country of origin. Students from the EU are treated as 'home students', but students from, for example, the United States have to pay much higher fees.

There has been an attempt to test the question whether it might be indirect discrimination against racial minorities to charge higher fees to overseas students (*Orphanos v Queen Mary College, London* [1985] 2 WLR 703). In *Orphanos*, which reached the House of Lords, a Cypriot student entered Queen Mary College, London, in 1982, to do mechanical engineering. The question was whether there was racial discrimination in expecting him to pay at the overseas rate. What was being tested was whether non-EEC nationals are a 'racial group' within the meaning of the Race Relations Act 1976.

---

25 27 June 1996, to UKCOSA.

A student's 'country of origin' may be a vexed question if he has parents of different nationalities and has lived in a series of different countries, perhaps even in the United Kingdom, during the period of his secondary education. A student who wants to claim that he is really a UK student may have to establish that he has a 'relevant connection' with the United Kingdom, which will usually depend on residence and exclude residence which was solely for the purpose of education. In other words, 'relevant connection' is not established just by sending someone to school in the United Kingdom.

Then there is the question of 'ordinary residence'. Lord Scarman defined 'ordinary residence' in *Shah v London Borough of Barnet* [1983] All ER 226, in terms of residing 'for a settled purpose'.[26] As is often the case, a ruling from a court may lead to statutory or regulatory change designed to frustrate it (making something which has just been defined as 'against the law' no longer against the law because the law has been changed). The result was a redrafting of the Education (Mandatory Awards) Regulations 1982 (as amended) Regulation 13, to state that an applicant is not to be treated as ordinarily resident if he came to the UK to gain full-time education. This case left room for challenge where there have been temporary absences abroad.

The fee difference at stake in *Orphanos* was considerable: £3,600 was at that time the fee for overseas students and £480 for home students. The scale of the difference is still great. There are cases where a student's nationality or fulfilment of the prior residence requirement may be in doubt; universities have been known to promise by mistake to take the student as a UK student and then to seek to exact fees at the overseas rate.

Continuing education

Students enrolled for courses in continuing education are not all in the same position. There is an enormous range of 'continuing education' courses, some offering no formal qualification at all because they are really offered as leisure activities. An example might be a weekend course in watercolour painting. Toward the other end of the spectrum are courses designed to prepare mature students who have become out of practice in

---

26 See Milman, D (1986) *Educational Conflict and the Law,* Croom Helm, London, p 105 and *R v Barnet LBC ex parte Shah* [1983] 2 WLR 16 at 32.

writing essays for university entrance, courses that would have a serious educational purpose but would not themselves be university courses. Further along still are courses leading to vocational qualifications or run in some conjoined way with departments of a university. Cambridge's Board of Continuing Education, for example, 'enrols' its students. They do courses that may lead to certificates, diplomas, advanced diplomas; they may work for a Certificate of Continuing Education or a Certificate of Higher Education, which carry credits that can be transferred within the Higher Education Credit Accumulation and Transfer scheme. It is possible to win enough of these to transfer in exchange for a whole year or half a year of a degree (but not a Cambridge degree, because Cambridge accepts no such credits).

One test is whether becoming a student involves 'enrolment' (anyone may come and there is no entrance test of qualification requirement) or 'admission' (only those selected as having the right qualifications and being capable of benefiting from the course may join it). Admission will normally make a student a member of the university, whereas a student on a continuing education course for which he has simply enrolled will not become a member.[27] Another test is whether the qualification offered at the end of the course is a degree or a degree-level qualification of a type that can be awarded only by an institution with the legal powers to award degrees. The 'rights' of an applicant to join the course are different. Fees are at the discretion of the university running continuing education courses.

Taking credit with you

It used to be customary for a student who went to a university to stay there until he or she had completed his or her degree. That is no longer universal and the widespread introduction of 'modules' has altered the assumption that a degree is a coordinated 'whole' that cannot easily be chopped up into parts and studied for at a series of institutions, one after the other.

Transferred credits are a relatively new phenomenon in higher education. A student may ask for admission to one institution after spending some time at another, and want to bring with him or her credits for the

27 On membership, see pp 37–38.

work he or she has already done, or seek just to be given recognition for a year or two spent somewhere else.

Each university has a right to accept or ignore any qualifications or credits the student already has. It will keep a list of institutions whose credits or partial qualifications it recognizes and will allow to count towards the final result in its own degree course. Fees would be payable to the university where the credit was obtained, in the usual way.

Postgraduate admissions

Postgraduate admissions constitute a further category with its own rules about the payment of fees. The range of postgraduate degrees available has expanded immensely in recent years with implications for admissions that have not yet really begun to be explored. But there are warning signals, especially about the huge expansion of taught 'master's' courses. For example, the *Times Higher Education Supplement* of 8 October 1999 reported a warning from its pro-vice-chancellor that, at Middlesex University Business School, 'students who fail a named master's award have been offered a multidisciplinary master's award...the clear implication is that the university runs two standards of master's programmes. This is indefensible'.

The picture used to be relatively simple, with a relatively clear distinction between research (PhD) and 'taught' courses (shorter 'taught'courses typically leading to a Master's degree). But a pattern of non-completion of PhDs and a rapidly expanding market for 'taught' Master's qualifications has led to a proliferation of both 'research' *and* 'taught' postgraduate degrees. There are now more 'taught' graduate courses, including 'taught' doctorates. A new kind of hurdle now exists at the stage when a student on an MPhil course sought admission to registration for a PhD. This is still largely untested ground, because students on MPhil courses may be admitted on the understanding that they wish eventually to do a PhD, and they are then seeking only to be 'transferred' from one course to another and not, strictly, to be 'admitted'. The situation is confusing.

Postgraduate funding has always been competitive and applicants have outnumbered the available grants. Science studentships are normally in the gift of a head of department, which can create a problem of 'patronage'.

Staff or student?

An unusual situation can arise when a postgraduate student is offered some teaching, or even a teaching post, in conjunction with the graduate studentship. There may be no commitment on the side of the institution and usually this works quite well from the point of view of the student, because the student gains experience that may help later in obtaining an academic teaching post and the money is also useful. Occasionally such arrangements can cause resentment because a student who is not given such teaching opportunities may complain that another student is being given an unfair advantage. In one case a Canadian student was 'formally' offered an appointment as 'a graduate teaching assistant' for three years, with a salary, and an arrangement that, in return, her tuition fees as a graduate student would be waived. There was a contract of employment. However, it turned out that the PhD that she had come to England to do could not be completed in that university because a particular programme was not available. It proved to be possible to have her studentship transferred elsewhere but it took many years of perseverance with the dispute before she received financial compensation and an apology from the university, which acknowledged that 'errors were made...which led to a graduate teaching assistantship being offered which was not fully in accordance with...representations. The University recognizes that it fell short...of the high standards it sets itself'.

This does not mean that all such offers are suspect, but it does mean that the student who is also going to be an employee has to be quite clear about the terms and the frame of reference.

Student action checklist

- ✔ Read the prospectus carefully.
- ✔ Also read all the accompanying documents/handbooks/leaflets about the course that you may be given before you arrive or at induction. Keep them carefully as a point of reference and a reminder of the promises made to you. It is important to keep the prospectus and handouts for the actual year when you began. Courses may change for subsequent years and the promises you should be able to rely on are the ones in force in the year you began.

- ✔ Make a note of any promises made to you at an open day or an interview about anything of particular importance to you in connection with the course. If you choose a course for a specific element in a syllabus, for example, you should be able to rely on that being provided.
- ✔ It is sensible to confirm in a letter when you accept a place what you understood you were told at interview or at an open day. That helps to avoid doubt if there is any difficulty later.
- ✔ As a general rule, put all important communications with the university, including telephone calls, in writing either at the time or as soon as possible afterwards. That too helps to avoid doubt if there is any difficulty later.
- ✔ If you find any 'disclaimers', saying that the university will not be responsible if there are changes to what it had promised, ask what that means.
- ✔ Ask about equal opportunities policies (sexual, racial, disability discrimination).
- ✔ Ask about equal access policies (public schools/state schools, bursaries and scholarships).
- ✔ Ask about the flexibility of arrangements. Can you change to part-time status part way through the course? Can you transfer 'credits' in and out of the university? Which other institutions does it recognize for this purpose?
- ✔ Ask whether your university is an 'old' or a 'new' (post-1992) one, whether you will become a 'member' as well as a student, whether there is a visitor.
- ✔ Ask exactly what you have to do to comply with the admission requirements, by way of the payment of fees and any other charges.
- ✔ Documents about or receipts for payment of fees should also be kept safely in case of any dispute. You will be surprised how often disputes about payments of fees arise.

2

The contract with the university

Admission

When a university or college offers a place and the prospective student accepts it, and pays fees, a contract is created. That may turn out to be the case even when an offer is made by someone who did not have authority to make it. The institution may have to admit the student who relied on that promise.[1]

It is now possible that if a student is admitted 'online' or by completion of forms elsewhere in the European Union there could be a 'cooling-off period' under EU Directive 97/07, implemented in the United Kingdom in June 2000. The student could probably cancel the contract and decide not to come. The situation where a 'tout' has claimed to represent the university and persuaded the student to sign up is more complex because much would depend on the authorization that he had to 'represent' the university.

Like all contracts, this is a *mutual* bargain, in which both parties give an undertaking, and the contract continues as long as both sides do what they have agreed to do. Something has already been said about the restrictions on universities making contracts with students in which they exploit their stronger position.[2] In any contract there are elements of 'trust' and 'mutual obligations', and in the obligation to preserve those things, both sides are

1 *Freeman v Lockyer and Buckhurst Park Properties* [1964] 2 QB 480; *Times Education Supplement*, 7 October 1983; *The Guardian*, 25 October 1983.

2 See p 11.

equal. That means the parties have to act in good faith towards one another and carry out the contract faithfully. This creates an obligation for the university and the student alike not to conduct themselves in a manner calculated or likely to destroy or seriously damage the relation of confidence and trust.[3]

This is the way in which an employment contract would be seen but there is a tendency to think in terms of a different type of contract in higher education: a 'service' contract, in which the university is offering something that resembles 'goods' or a 'product' (education, a degree course) and the student is a 'consumer'. It is from the basic requirements of this sort of contract that there derives an obligation for a university to come up with what it has promised to deliver.

Conditions of acceptance

When a student accepts a place he or she is deemed to agree to the 'conditions of acceptance', which include paying the fees and keeping the rules and may include other points. An offer of a place may be conditional or unconditional and if there are conditions attached to the offer the full contract does not come into being until they have been fulfilled. For example, if a student is asked for certain grades at A level but does not get them, the university does not *have* to accept the student (although it may, if it chooses, still give him or her a place).

A contract may not be 'complete' unless and until the conditions laid down are satisfied. In *D v Queen's University of Belfast* [1997] ELR 431 CA (a case involving an employee, not a student) it was found that the very satisfaction of the conditions was part of the process of appointment.[4] The same thing would in principle presumably apply to a student contract.

In *Moran v University College, Salford* [1994] ELR CA at 199 the role of the PCAS (the then Polytechnics Central Admissions System) came into the picture. Even though the actual 'agency' has changed, this case needs to be borne in mind, because the actual offers of places still come to students

3 Cf. *University of Nottingham v Eyert and the Pensions Ombudsman* [1999] ELR 141.

4 The question at issue here was whether or not termination before probation ends is in the ordinary sense a dismissal.

from an intermediate agency, UCAS. The student was made an offer that he accepted and the court agreed that 'there was an agreement...formed through the agency of the PCAS'.[5] The university tried to argue that no agreement existed 'until such time as the student-applicant enrols and is accepted as such'. This case was important in testing the principle that a contract comes into being on the 'offer' of a place and not only at the point where the student enrols or registers and actually becomes a student, and also that it can come into being if an agent or representative makes the offer and informs the university that the offer has been made.

That leads on to the question of the duties that a university has to clarify the 'conditions' of a 'conditional' offer, because they may go far beyond obtaining particular qualifications. One student sought to bring an action against a college of further education for breach of contract over the college's alleged failure to clarify what was required as a condition of entry. It was alleged that she had failed to declare previous 'convictions' on a police check form provided by the college. She had had a 'caution' from the police but it was merely a caution. The notes of guidance in the Standards of Conduct Expected of Students in the College set out no criteria that would have required 'cautions' to be declared.

That is a good example of the problem that a university may have unclear rules, or rules in small print, or rules that the student does not see, and may be told about in passing without the student really understanding their purpose or force. That can cover promises as well as warnings. There have been cases where prospective overseas students have been assured by a university's agent that students who do not speak English will be given full support, and have arrived to find that they are left to flounder.[6]

For all these reasons, the promises or warnings made on behalf of a college or university may be binding even if they are not in writing. It is sensible to keep a note of anything merely 'said' with the date and the name of the person who said it. The ground rules are not difficult to sum up.

The university agrees to act fairly and reasonably, that is:

---

5 Even though 'PCAS had no authority to enter into legal relations on behalf of the respondent, his acceptance was in fact notified to the respondents'.

6 Elaine Maxwell, 'The University Contract', RAWS Conference, Sheffield, 24 March, 1999.

- to admit the student if the fee is paid and the student keeps the rules;
- to allow the student to do the course that is specified, and to provide that course as promised;
- to provide the student with satisfactory teaching and adequate facilities to enable him or her to do the course;
- to examine the student, so that if he or she fulfils the requirements he or she can gain a qualification.

A model contract

THIS IS AN AGREEMENT between [...] hereinafter called 'the institution' and ... hereinafter called 'the student'.

The Institution undertakes that in consideration of the payment of its stipulated tuition fees by or on behalf of the student and the due observance by the student of the provisions of [the Institution's Charter and Statutes/Instrument and Articles of Government, Ordinances/Byelaws, Regulations and Rules] as are current during the period of this Agreement [and are set out in the Calendar] it will provide adequate tuition and supervision of professional quality in respect of a programme of study leading to the degree or other qualification for which the student has been admitted and is registered subject to the following conditions:

(i) the student must achieve and sustain such standards of academic performance as are stipulated by the Institution from time to time in respect of the programme being followed and the Institution undertakes not to change such standards unilaterally without prior consultation with the student or student representatives;

(ii) the Institution reserves the right upon giving notice which is reasonable in all the circumstances to make changes in the programme of courses being offered for reasons of changes in funding, in staffing or for any other reasonable cause;

(iii) the student submits to the jurisdiction of the Institution in matters connected with academic progress and discipline while on Institution premises or engaged in Institution activities and the Institution agrees that the exercise of that jurisdiction shall be subject to standards of reasonableness and fairness.

The Institution and the student agree that the terms of this Agreement shall prevail over the content of any prospectus or other similar marketing

> material, or any written or oral statement made by either party or by the Institution's employees or agents.
>
> Any disputes arising from the interpretation or performance of this Agreement and which cannot be resolved by negotiation between the parties shall be referred for decision by the University's visitor [an arbitrator shall be appointed on a standing basis by the Institution and the Students' Association] and such decision shall be final and binding on both parties.
>
> (Farrington, D J (1998) *The Law of Higher Education*, 2nd edn, Butterworth, London, pp 402–03)

Learner agreements, codes of practice and codes of good supervisory practice embodying these principles ought to be available from any university.

Enrolment, registration, matriculation

When the student arrives at the university there is usually a transaction or formal exchange consisting of the payment of the fee and some sort of admission procedure, for in order to become a student the applicant must 'enrol', 'register' or 'matriculate'. The first two place the student on a list. Matriculation does something else as well, by making the student a member of the university.[7]

Registration may also be different from enrolment. This distinction has been used by at least one university that seems to have been trying to evade a commitment. In one case overseas students at one of the 'new' London universities who had transferred with their research supervisor from another institution could not continue as students there when their supervisor had his contract terminated during the probationary period. The university then disowned them. This created some international furore and did the reputation of British universities harm on the Indian subcontinent. The university acknowledged that the students had been 'enrolled', but it denied that they had been 'registered' and on that basis it sought to deny that there had been any contract. The case was not pursued through the courts, so an opportunity was lost to test the distinction and see whether it

7 That tends to apply in 'old' universities. See *Moran v University College Salford* (1993) *The Times*, 23 November and Maxwell, 'The University Contract'.

would hold in contract law. The accepted view is that some consideration of monetary value would pass from the student to the university as part of the intention to create legal relations, but the payment of the fee was not at issue here.

A further student was caught in this same trap, in the same episode. He came from the Republic of Ireland and consequently he was an EU student whose loss over the fees was less substantial. The university made the curious gesture of offering him accommodation in one of its halls to the value of the £3,000 he was claiming he had lost in the form of a year's fees. He had by then found a college in the 'old' University of London to take him. The geographical position of the accommodation offered was a long way from where he now needed to live. He refused the offer and things rested there, so once more the principle was not tested.

Registration may be a single act covering all the years of the course (especially in the traditional single-subject type of course) or the student may be registered on a year-by-year basis (especially for modular courses). There may be a requirement to pass the examination that is set at each stage of the course before proceeding to the next, and in that case the registration might be repeated year by year.

However it is marked or sealed, there is a defining moment when no one can dispute that a contract has come into being between the university and the student, something which is more than a basic promise to admit him to the course in return for his promise to pay the fees and so on.

After the contract has been 'made' at the registration of the student, any change in it should have the consent of the student as well as the institution. That might still allow the institution to make changes to the courses if the prospectus says it reserves that right. Again, part of the problem is that the partners to this contract are unequal in their power to strike a bargain. The university can in reality make its own terms and say to the student 'take it or leave it'.

In one example, a student argued that there was breach of contract for failure to provide proper teaching and adequate facilities. The student, who had not yet finished her course, had spent money on providing for herself facilities that should have been provided by the institution. This was a highly specialized course, and it was not easy for her to find an equivalent elsewhere. She did in the end discover a possibility but she needed two consents before she could transfer. The first institution had to give its permission and the local education authority had to give its consent to the transfer of her fees to the new 'course provider'. The first university tried to stipulate that they would provide such consent only if the student signed a disclaimer that she would not subsequently sue the university. She was able to resist this unfair term of the agreement only with legal advice and help, on the grounds of fairness and reasonableness, which are well-established legal territory.

This was a good example of the common sense of seeking legal advice in good time, when friendly negotiations do not work and especially if the university tries to use its institutional muscle to force the hand of the individual student. It is also an illustration of the need for perseverance. Universities can be slow and intransigent because they have much more time at their disposal than a student whose life and career may be on hold during a dispute.

Becoming a member of the university

In a 'chartered' university (founded pre-1992), or in Oxford or Cambridge, the student also becomes a 'corporator' or member. So not all students stand in the same relationship to their university and although they all have contracts with their university, some have rights and responsibilities as 'members' and others do not.

The idea of membership derives from the ancient notion that a university is a guild, to which scholars belong for life. They are 'incorporated' – that is, made members of a 'body'. That is why the duration of membership of Oxford and Cambridge Colleges and of these Universities is perpetual. Someone who has graduated from Oxford or Cambridge[8] is a 'senior member' forever, with enduring rights to use the library. Senior and junior membership originated in a relatively straightforward distinction between the 'apprentices' or 'journeymen' and the 'masters', who, together with other masters, formed the guild itself. A degree certificate admitting to the Oxford MA still refers to 'the Register of the Ancient House of Congregation of Doctors and Regent Masters of the University of Oxford'.

There have been attempts to draw together these categories of

8 Provided he or she had proceeded to the MA degree.

'contractual' and 'membership' relationship, and to suggest that they are really the same thing. It has been suggested that there may be a 'contract of membership' that entitles a student to be treated in accordance with the university's rules but, for practical purposes, the most important thing for students is that membership is taken to bind them to obey the 'domestic laws' of the university. In being legally 'domestic', a university is like a 'club'.[9] That is an important difference because, whereas the courts will take an interest in breach of contract, they will be reluctant to interfere in the private affairs of such a 'domestic' forum.[10] On the other hand, it can now be argued that a university has a 'public' function; it receives, even depends on, public funds, and that may make a difference to the ground rules in the future.

Student action checklist

- ✔ What is the university's policy about seeking to withhold degrees from students who have not paid their bills?
- ✔ Does it distinguish between payment of tuition fees and payment of bills for accommodation and payment of any fines?
- ✔ Are these policies published?
- ✔ Are students made aware of them?

9 In *R v University of Aston, ex parte Roffey* [1969] membership of a university was said to be 'akin to membership of a social body'.

10 See pp 87–90 and pp 125–30.

3

Taking care of students: welfare and safety

> James...is in a Hall of residence which is being extended; unfortunately the building work has dragged on into Term and now the entire hot-water/heating system has packed up; the Hall Manager hopes things will improve next week...James, in an attempt to keep warm, acquires a paraffin heater; the Hall Manager, with whom his relationship is now a little strained, finds the heater and a gallon of paraffin in a plastic container in his room, packs up the student's belongings and dumps them on the Hall steps.[1]

Universities owe students a duty of care. They must provide a safe place for the provision of education. A university's duty of care extends to making sure that students are not in danger. The university has to make reasonable efforts to keep its students safe. When a student reading forestry at the University of Edinburgh fell from a tree he was awarded compensation of more than £112,000.[2]

There is no duty to take more than 'reasonable' care. For example, if the student is a known carrier of infection the institution has responsibilities to other students and staff to ensure that they are placed in no danger, but that duty would begin only when it knew of the infection. This is in line with the principle that the university may not be liable for the actions of students

1 This fictional example is used with grateful acknowledgement to David Palfreyman, who provided it for an OECD Conference at New College, Oxford, 20–22 September 1999.
2 *Tuttle v University of Edinburgh* [1984] SLT (OH) 172.

that cause damage to others, because it cannot be expected to control everything they do.

A claim on behalf of a group of Westminster University students about lack of central heating and hot water in their hall of residence was successful in persuading the university to settle out of court. A university might have a duty to supervise a gymnastics facility. A university student suffered serious injury as a result of doing a forward somersault without supervision in the activities room of Bedford Youth House, which was owned and occupied by Bedfordshire County Council. In this case the responsible body was not a university, but the rule would still apply if it had been.[3]

Physical injury is easily proved, but it has now been established that injury may be psychological as well as physical,[4] so a university might be liable for that kind of damage to a student if it did not make reasonable provision to protect against it. Most universities have counselling services that, if properly run, would afford that kind of protection.

The university has to make sure students can work in peace. That is another type of 'welfare' duty. In *Smith v Nottinghamshire County Council, The Times*, 13 November 1981 it was held that a student was entitled to quiet in which to revise for his examinations. The *Times Higher Education Supplement* of 12 July 1996 carried the story of a threat of legal action by students because of course disruption from building work. The first edition of *The Cambridge Student* in October 1999 carried a note of concern about the massive and prolonged noisy building operations affecting a high proportion of students in the humanities.

Health and safety legislation includes the Health and Safety at Work Act (1974) and the Occupier's Liability Act (1975) and there may also be a liability in tort, so universities need to set up their provisions for taking care of student welfare on a broad basis.

Disabled students

'Skill' is the national bureau for students with disabilities (Chapter House, 18–20 Crucifix Lane, London, SE1 3JW, 020 7450 0620; www.skill.org.uk).

3 *Fowles v Bedfordshire County Council* [1996] ELR 51.
4 *Walker v Northumberland County Council* [1995] ELR 231.

The Disability Discrimination Act of 1995 is a more recent piece of legislation than the sex and race discrimination legislation and its implications are still being thought through. The provision of educational services is currently exempt but many of the 'services' that a university provides are not directly or strictly 'educational' and may fall under the requirements of the Act. Legislation to cover educational provision is imminent. Consultation on the Disability Rights in Education Bill has been completed and the key points to emerge are that it will become unlawful for education providers to fail to make a reasonable adjustment where any arrangements, including the physical features of premises, place disabled students at a disadvantage in comparison to non-disabled students. It will also become unlawful for students unjustifiably to be treated less favourably for a reason related to their disability.

Redress will be through the County Court by way of financial compensation. There will be a clearer definition of the circumstances in which the education provider is deemed to know of the disability (if a member of staff is told or if it can reasonably be expected to know).

Increasingly, universities and colleges are emphasising the ways in which they cater for disabled students. Some define disability and specify the available facilities. Some have a disability adviser. The fact that these undertakings have been given can become important if the disabled student arrives to find that the facilities do not exist or that the promises have not been kept. One student came in a wheelchair to find that his dyslexia was not to be catered for although that was just as much a disability to him as a student as the condition that made him unable to walk.

There are special considerations for disabled students. There may be obvious practical reasons why a particular applicant cannot complete the course alongside other students. How far does a university have to go to ensure that the student can do so if it is at all possible?

Not all disabilities are visible. A student may have reasons for not wanting the university to know about his or her disability and has a right to privacy about it. He or she may tell the university about the disability and request that it is treated as confidential. In that case, the student has a right to know whether his or her tutors and teachers are to be told about it and to object if he or she does not wish that. Disabled students do not have to tell the university about their disability, but if they do not explain in advance the disadvantage it puts them under, the university has no duty to make adjustments to help them, although it will usually try to help.

The same problem may arise for students who are not disabled but merely temporarily unwell and who do not want to tell the university of their medical condition. A student who does not explain about an illness before taking an examination cannot usually mention it afterwards in an appeal about the outcome of the examination. For the student, there is a real dilemma here about confidentiality, and it is important to be aware of the consequences before deciding not to mention illness.

There are circumstances in which there may be an obligation on a prospective student to tell the university about illness, for example, if it may affect others. 'Carriers' of HIV and infectious hepatitis and some other infections would have a duty to tell the university because that might affect the welfare of others. But they themselves might not be ill.

The Quality Assurance Agency (QAA) *Code of Practice: Students with disabilities* encourages institutions to make sure that disabled students can obtain access to course information and application details, in a form in which the students can read or take it in, as well as to the physical environment of the institution itself. There is an expectation that the applicant's views will be taken into consideration.

A number of areas are flagged up by the QAA 'disability' guidelines, which have tended to be neglected or left to chance by universities. For example, field trips and academic placements are especially difficult to arrange for wheelchair users; research students with disabilities may suffer potential disadvantages not faced by first-degree students because they may have to go into inaccessible places to gather their research materials.

Dyslexia

Dyslexia is a special problem for universities, because it affects students' capacity to express themselves on paper. It therefore goes to the heart of the work that students have to do to get a degree. It is an increasing problem, not only because more students are coming forward to say that their study difficulties arise from dyslexia but also because the scope of the problems now considered to be covered by dyslexia is enlarging. It is now accepted that it may cover not only a difficulty with spelling but also difficulties in putting thoughts in order or in expressing oneself clearly.

Those are failings for which examiners penalize students who are not dyslexic, so a student who claims dyslexia for the first time at university, when he has not said he was dyslexic at school, may be regarded with suspicion. Most universities will arrange for tests. The student may have to pay for such a test, both because large numbers asking for tests may be expensive for the university and also because that is seen as a discouragement to those who are just 'trying it on'.

There is an urgent need for training for those who have to deal with dyslexic candidates not only on admission but later in their courses. A chairman of examiners was sent a list of officially 'dyslexic' candidates in the summer of 2000. She was told that appropriate time allowances would need to be arranged. After a few days' thought she sent a puzzled e-mail, 'do you mean for us to mark them?' She had apparently no understanding of the spread of disadvantages that dyslexia is now recognized to include and it is unlikely that candidates whose papers she marked could have had a proper and appropriate allowance made for their disabilities because of their examiner's ignorance.

Dyslexia may be a complicating factor in a situation where something else has gone wrong in the relationship between the student and the institution. A disabled student with cerebral palsy and spinal injury, in a wheelchair, was offered a place at a new university, and a room in one of its halls of residence in September 1997. He attended the interview in his wheelchair so the university was certainly aware of his needs as a wheelchair user. At his interview he met the special needs coordinator and was assured that the university had good provisions to meet the needs of users of wheelchairs and that he would suffer no disadvantage.

He also told the university that he had dyslexia. It was not until he arrived that he learnt that he was not to be offered any help with his dyslexia until he had had an assessment. On 26 September 1997 the new arrival went to a dyslexic student formal presentation. He was informed that any assessment of special needs had to be logged by the fifth week of term. He knew that this could not be achieved in his case. He found that the university was not ready to discuss the assessment that he needed; a member of staff said she would not conduct the assessment herself because she might be held liable.

The university had a disability statement in which it said that it was committed to:

- promoting access for all who can benefit including those for whom Higher Education has traditionally not been accessible;
- encouraging equality of opportunity;
- eliminating unfair discrimination in recruitment and admissions processes and in assessment decisions.

So he was not provided with the facilities that he needed as a disabled student. He felt that he was not able to begin his course. If he was able to show that that was indeed the case and that it was the university's fault, his breach of contract case against the first university would involve damages that included compensation for his considerable expenditure on the special equipment he needed because of his disability, and the fact that he was left with only the option of taking his degree through the Open University, which would take him four years and so lose him two years' earnings.

In this story the dyslexia was only an element but it proved to be a trigger factor in creating a situation in which this student could not go on with his course.

In another case the additional factors were not themselves to do with disability, but once more the presence of a problem about dyslexia led to disaster for the student. A student sought legal aid in connection with a dispute over a course for the diploma in social work. She was a satisfactory student and there were no problems until her second year. She had a degree of dyslexia, although it had not previously prevented her completing her coursework satisfactorily.

It was at that stage an essential integral part of the course that she should undertake a 'placement'. This student complained formally to the programme director about problems she was experiencing and although she tried to continue she eventually gave up and left the placement. She wrote to request that she be allowed to 'defer' for the year and begin again in September. The college told her that she must 'withdraw'. She would then have to reapply for the second year of the course and to undergo an interview at which her 'learning needs' (in relation to the dyslexia) would be discussed. When she did that she was told that she could not be readmitted because she had not worked out a means of dealing with the difficulties caused by her dyslexia. She appealed against this decision and the appeal was rejected. She was left without qualification, without a job, and being asked to repay several hundred pounds which was part of her original grant.

Did the college break its contract with this student? She believed that it failed to give her an appropriate placement, which would allow her to comply with the requirements of the college's assessment criteria. The suggested claim was for specific performance to get her readmitted to complete her studies and damages for the money she had had to repay for her grant and also for the lost opportunity of obtaining work in her chosen career.

So it is important for students with disabilities to clarify their position at the outset and to ensure that the university has its procedures and its thoughts in order.

Mental health

The CVCP Guidelines on Student Mental Health Policies and Procedures for Higher Education were issued in April 2000. The guidelines recognize the complexity of this area and the overlap of medical with 'social, personal, economic and environmental factors'. Student life is increasingly stressful; students now have to cope not only with the traditional pressures of living independently from their parents for the first time, but also with debt and the need to earn money while studying. A high proportion of those reporting problems in this area spoke of depression; another large group of anxiety or panic attacks; another substantial proportion – almost half of the respondents to one survey – said they had problems with self-esteem and confidence.

The new guidelines recognize that the problems are now of a kind and on a scale where institutions need specialist help and ought not routinely to leave it to untrained academics to offer 'pastoral care' for everyone. A term is implied in all contracts for the provision of services that the supplier will supply the services with reasonable skill and care (Supply of Goods and Services Act, 1982, s13). So if a university provides counselling services, for example, it imposes a duty upon itself to do it properly – that is, with reasonable skill as well as with reasonable care. This contractual duty of care also requires the institution to be careful when it admits a student to give the student the opportunity to ask about any reasonably foreseeable special needs the student is likely to have for counselling or support of this sort.

An area of difficulty arises where a student is unwilling to agree that he or she has a mental health problem. There are potential nightmare scenarios here, where the student could be put under unacceptable pressure to 'medicalize' a perfectly normal but inconvenient personality trait. Human rights issues are likely to present themselves here. 'Obtaining psychiatric help' should not be made a condition of being allowed to complete a degree.

A student exhibiting disturbed behaviour might well find him- or herself under discipline. That could be inappropriate if the student was really suffering mental health problems for which the university had a duty to provide him or her with help rather than punishment.

Students need good access to lists of bodies and services that can help them, including those that are outside the university such as local mental health care teams. In fact a comprehensive directory of all the possibilities needs to be in the hands of everyone in the institution.

Training sessions for staff can include students too, so that the culture and climate of the institution includes 'being well informed' about the clues to look for and the effects on others in the community of mental disturbance in a student. It should be noted that members of staff may become mentally disturbed too, and that students may need protecting from the consequences of a depressed lecturer's failure to mark their essays, and so on.

Confidentiality issues are going to arise with particular force in areas where a student is naturally sensitive about having the nature (or the very existence) of mental health difficulties communicated to those who teach him or her or to fellow students. Yet someone has to keep an eye on a student who has tried to commit suicide. In what circumstances will parents be contacted? Is this stated in writing where every student can read what the relevant rules are?

Both the CVCP guidelines and the QAA *Code of Practice: Students with disabilities* (1999) emphasize that a student suffering from mental health difficulties may need appropriate opportunities to take time off from study, or to reschedule part of the course. There may also be problems about the stress associated with certain methods of examination or assessment.

Practical requirements

For the issues outlined under all the above headings the institution ought to:

- train its staff;
- create adequate procedures;
- ensure that the procedures are followed;
- keep careful records of what happens in the handling of specific cases (records of which copies are given to the student affected).

Student action checklist

- ✔ Find out what published policies the university has about student welfare and safety.
- ✔ Are there student halls of residence belonging to and run by the university? What are the rules?
- ✔ Check the Equal Opportunities Policy.
- ✔ Is there a Disability Statement?
- ✔ Is there a policy about physical access for disabled students?
- ✔ Is there realistic provision for dealing with multiple health problems or problems emerging after a student has been admitted?
- ✔ Is there a code of practice about protecting the confidentiality of student information about long-term or short-term medical conditions?
- ✔ It is worth looking at the University Web sites for relevant sources of information.

4

Providing guidance and clear information about course and examination requirements

A university has an obligation to provide adequate guidance and feedback to its students to help them complete the course requirements. This includes informing them clearly about any rules that describe the consequences if they fail to meet any obligations or requirements during the course. In one recent case, an MPhil student was not warned that if she failed in her assessed essays early in the course she would not be allowed to continue.

The authority for this ruling was a Faculty memorandum, which had not been communicated to the students it affected. Its intention was benevolent; it was designed to save a student from wasting money in fees if he or she was doing so badly that there was no chance of obtaining the degree. But one term is not long to give a student to 'make good'; some students might do better in a second or third term and this device cut off their opportunity and denied them the right to choose to continue at their own risk.

There is a great deal of muddle in this area. Universities frequently make changes to rules and forget to tell students affected by those changes. A student adversely affected might be able to claim that he or she had had a reasonable expectation of being told certain things, which had been frustrated.

In any event, students should be advised to obtain all rules and regulations themselves and read them carefully. This is an important ground rule because it is not usually an acceptable defence to claim ignorance of the rules after something has gone wrong. Universities are quick to quote their rules and regulations when they make a decision. The university will often include the relevant rules in the student handbook, or make them available in the library. The student should ask to be told where the rules and regulations can be found and the university must then provide them or say where they are to be located.

It is also important for the student to get a copy of the set of rules and regulations in force at the date when the student began the course. Rules change a good deal, and the student needs to be clear which version applies in his or her own case.

Providing adequate teaching

James is accepted by Ludlow to read physics with metallurgy. He arrives in October only to be told that the metallurgy component of the joint degree can no longer be delivered because the relevant laboratory space has just been gutted by fire, or the six academics in the Department of Metallurgy had left over the summer to take jobs elsewhere, or the University of Ludlow had decided to make academics redundant to make savings. As his grades are too weak to be acceptable to physics for the single-honours course, he is told that Dr Sparky has helpfully arranged for him to register to do physics at Ipswich.[1]

If a student is paying fees he or she is entitled to 'value for money'. In the simplest terms this means that a university has an obligation to provide adequate teaching and adequate feedback to enable its students to prepare for, and take, their examinations. This is the normal 'vehicle' for the provision of courses.

It is an increasingly vexed area, with a high proportion of complaints from students citing poor or inadequate supervision. That can range from alleged lack of interest in or time spent with a student (especially a research student) to incompetence or lack of knowledge or qualifications on the part of university teachers. Or it could include not marking work, or not marking it thoroughly, or taking a very long time to mark it – all common failings. There is also a problem of promised courses not being available or expected supervisors having moved on.

---

1 This fictional example (adapted) is used with grateful acknowledgement to David Palfreyman, who provided it for an OECD Conference at New College, Oxford, 20–22 September 1999.

It is a surprisingly common complaint that a university has failed to deliver the set number of lectures, tutorials or seminars promised in the course syllabus. If that is because of illness, the university has a duty to make a reasonable attempt to cover for the missing lecturer. Sudden cancellations without notice or good reason are not acceptable. They may affect the quality of the course and raise the question of 'value for money'. If a driving instructor failed to turn up for a prearranged session, the learner driver would not be expected to pay for it.

A breach of contract case in this area arose out of a situation where the lecturer employed to teach mathematics and computers for a degree in computing and information systems was absent and no lectures at all took place for a period, except for a 10-minute performance by a substitute on one occasion. Seminars and tutorials that were essential to the course were cancelled without notice and not rescheduled. Work was not marked or assessed.

At this same college a lecturer pointed out that a question set in an examination for the degree course was taken from a previous A-level examination paper. Students reading that in *The Times* in February 1997 were naturally disturbed; it threw into question the standard of the course they were on.

It is not clear whether the practice of using graduate students to teach in place of more senior members of staff would necessarily come under this heading. Some graduate students are first-rate supervisors and teachers and give more time and effort to preparation than their seniors.

The Dearing Report pressed for improvement in teaching standards and it proposed to set up a new professional body known as the Institute for Learning and Teaching. This may eventually help to clarify the standard of teaching provision that students may reasonably expect.

There has been an expectation shift towards the idea that the burden is not all on the student to work hard and learn, but also on the university to 'prepare' and 'equip' the student to pass the examination. Twenty years ago research students largely expected to work on their own, at least in the humanities. Now they are offered taught courses at MPhil level to prepare them for research.[2] This is partly a reflection of changes in the same direction in patterns of teaching in secondary schools and the different needs of the higher proportion of the population that now goes on to higher education. It is now no longer clear where a reasonable balance lies. But a student

2 See pp 27–28.

who did not go to the lectures or classes provided and did not do the work required could not complain that it was the university's fault he or she failed an examination.

What is good teaching?

So what is good teaching? It can be divided into delivery and content. Under both heads, the teacher's job is to ensure that the student receives effective and timely help to understand and to learn. The content should be adequate, well presented and clear. Teaching should be interesting, with a measure of excitement.

All of this could be required of school teaching as well as of university teaching. Is there a difference? It is still largely unclear in what respects if any a teacher in higher education needs different skills from those of a teacher in a school. Some skills are straightforward. Knowing one's subject and being able to explain it clearly are obviously good things, on any definition of good teaching. Being able to interest and hold an audience is also important (not being dull, inaudible). However, the powers of a first-rate teacher go beyond that, in awakening long-term interest in the listener or creating intellectual excitement, for example. In university teaching there should be something more, glimpses of the 'cutting edge' of research or the boundaries of present knowledge. The student should be shown something of the wider intellectual world in which scholars can spend a lifetime exploring a single problem and never exhaust it.

University teachers used to be free to branch out along a new path or to stop in the middle of a lecture when a new, perhaps creative idea struck them, and explore it on the spot. They could set essays (in agreement with their students) on subjects that the student found particularly interesting. Students might turn over an examination paper in the examination room and find questions that tested the independent reading it would be assumed that they had done. It was seen as of the essence of *higher* education that it took the student into areas where not many people had gone before and that they were learning how to learn for themselves.

Few university teachers possess a formal teaching qualification. That came about because they had often spent several years after they graduated doing a research degree whereas those going on to teach in schools had done a teaching qualification 'instead'. Since the Dearing Report there has been a growing expectation that teachers in higher education will join the Institute of Learning and Teaching.

The orthodoxy from the late 1990s required something more predictable. This may restrict the 'stars', in the interests of ensuring an adequate general standard of teaching across the board in universities. It has also encouraged a certain style of teaching, where everything is clearly mapped and the student knows in advance what is due to be taught each week. This is appropriate and helpful in some subjects. In many of the humanities it is not. It may be counterproductive in a subject whose essence is debate (such as philosophy) or for a teacher who is actively engaged in research in the area where he or she is teaching and wants to be able to convey to students the excitement of the chase or an understanding of what he or she has just learned. In something of this spirit, the Privy Council has recently refused to allow a university to change its statutes to include the word 'training', on the grounds that universities provide education not training.

Students are now entitled to receive a clear idea of what is expected of them and what they have to learn. If the institution promises a course containing particular elements, those elements have to be taught.

The Higher Education Funding Council has done a survey and has drawn up five 'national priorities'. The first is to ensure that 'learning and teaching' provision recognizes the diverse needs of the institution's students. The second emphasizes staff development. The third seeks to promote innovation in the curriculum, particularly activity associated with employability. Then there is 'transferring and adopting good practices in learning and teaching' and 'exploitation of communications and information technology' (HEFCE Council Briefing, May 2000).

Teaching quality assurance has involved a great deal of 'inspection'. Most departments have achieved very creditable gradings and academics have been quick to learn how to present their teaching practices to the TQA visitors so as to fit the requirements with which they are presented. A drawback of all this is that it has been geared to gradings or rankings, for public consumption in league tables, rather than to improving the quality of teaching that is really being provided. Yet students in high-rating departments still complain of the sort of 'student neglect' (failure to mark essays in reasonable time, lack of opportunities to talk through their difficulties) that may matter most to the ordinary student.

The student who feels he or she is not getting sufficient, or sufficiently good, teaching will have to wrestle with these questions, which are actively exercising everyone in higher education at present. Lack of teaching, or neglecting to mark essays, is clearly a breach of the contract with the student on the part of the institution. Provision of a given type of teaching or style of teaching may not be.

A largely untested area at the time of writing is the provision of courses on the Internet. There has been strong government pressure to encourage this, but it may be much harder to show that there has been a failure of a proper standard of provision. A number of questions arise about 'admission' to such courses and about the conduct of examinations and the award of degrees by an 'e-university' or by conventional universities 'using' or 'providing' such courses.

Providing adequate facilities

History can be taught without Bunsen burners, but chemistry cannot. Under provision of 'facilities' will come libraries, laboratories, equipment appropriate to those subjects for which it is needed. A university has a duty not to offer courses for which it cannot provide such facilities as are indispensable for completing the course. For example, it could not reasonably offer science degrees if it had no laboratories at all. In one case a college provided only a room with plastic flooring for a course in which welding was an essential component. There must also be adequate access (*enough* facilities).

It is a problem for universities that some subjects can be taught more cheaply than others, and sometimes differential course fees reflect that difference of expense. A university could argue that that was reasonable. On the other hand, postgraduate students in the arts and humanities, especially those from overseas, are increasingly complaining that they do not get their money's worth for the many thousands of pounds of their fees, when all they are given is the occasional hour with a single supervisor and access to the library.

The duty to provide facilities may go beyond academic provision, but it is not clear how far. In Cambridge the question of the provision of a prayer room for Moslem students to use at midday became contentious in 1999 when it was pointed out that general washrooms were being used to wash feet before praying, offending other users, and the university wanted the room back for other uses anyway. At that point it began to be argued that equivalent provision was not being made for those of other faiths. This may not be a matter directly related to provision of facilities for learning, but for a devout Moslem such facilities could be important to the successful completion of the course. How far does the duty to provide facilities extend?

Maintaining standards

The university has to provide an education of a satisfactory standard. This is a different kind of obligation from the others we have examined so far. In a sense, it overarches them all because it includes them all. The most helpful idea, in the terms of the 'consumer contract' model of the relationship between the university and the student, may be the former concept of 'merchandisable quality', now known as 'satisfactory quality'.

There is little or no case law on 'academic' standards, because, as we shall see, the courts have been reluctant to interfere with academic judgements.[3] However, a distinction can be drawn between what may be called a 'contractual' standard – that is, a reasonable standard of provision – and the more esoteric idea of an 'academic standard', which is not just a measure of quantitative adequacy but the promise to make available something altogether richer and harder to measure.

Universities are under great pressure to produce results, and that may not be to the benefit of students if it encourages them to alter grades, raise marks, give more first-class degrees, and so debase the achievements of their students in the public eye. It puts the emphasis on things that are relatively easier to measure. Individual students may be anxious about the opposite possibility, that their marks may have been lowered to fit a 'profile'. From time to time examples of alleged tinkering with examination marks for reasons that are not purely academic emerge into the light of day, and students are entitled to appeal if they have reason to believe that that has happened.[4]

---

3 See pp 68–70.

4 The *Times Higher Education Supplement* of 31 October 1997 carried the story of instructions to assessors at Thames Valley University to treat marks of 30 per cent in September resits as though they had been marks of 40 per cent.

In 1998 the new Quality Assurance Agency produced a Code of Practice for the Assurance of Academic Quality and Standards in Higher Education: Postgraduate Research Programmes. The text had a double thrust. The first was the requirement that 'full and part-time research programmes will only be offered where students can be expected to meet the academic standards the institution has set for itself, which should reflect national expectations' (1A). This is puzzling until it emerges that the purpose is to prevent universities that are keen to maintain numbers from admitting students who are not likely to be fitted for research. The second main idea is that there should be a duty upon the university to ensure that it makes the necessary provision to make possible the successful completion of student research. 'Supervisors should possess recognized subject expertise' (9A); '[s]upervisors should have the necessary skills and experience to monitor, support and direct research students' work' (9B).

The whole quality assurance programme is still in its infancy. The first documents to be produced by the QAA, for example in 'subject benchmarking' tend to be general and they merely underline the difficulty of ensuring that students receive good teaching and high-quality courses in the wide range of institutions and subjects that are now on offer. Accordingly, a huge amount of effort has recently been put into the development of subject benchmarks. The QAA engaged in an extended consul- tation for the purpose, to try to ensure that it was reflecting the reality.

The notion of benchmarks has a number of drawbacks. One is that the creation of benchmarks for specific subjects makes the assumption that subjects form discrete disciplines each with its own distinctive qualities and excellences. That makes it difficult for courses that cross boundaries and experiment with new ideas to meet these rather fixed standards, which may be only partly appropriate. The benchmark approach may also place a constraint upon teaching.

The best thing for students themselves to do when they want to raise questions is probably to concentrate on the obvious indicators that the provision is not satisfactory – failures to cover all the topics in the course; failures of lecturers to be clear and comprehensible, or to turn up at all. Those are good places to start and enquiries may lead on from there to bring about a general improvement.

Student action checklist

- ✔ Make sure you have asked for copies of all regulations in force.
- ✔ Check that there have been no changes before you take any examinations, and ask that all students be given copies of any changes made by those teaching or running the course.
- ✔ It is reasonable to complain if several lectures or seminars are not provided or if work is not marked at all or if facilities really needed for the course are not provided. This should not extend to complaining because a lecturer's 'style' is not liked.
- ✔ Similarly, it is reasonable to complain if the university has failed to fulfil any promise made to the students.
- ✔ Make the complaint in moderate language and try to get a group of the students affected to sign it.
- ✔ Ask the student union to endorse the complaint.
- ✔ Students can ask the university for a 'plan of action' to remedy any particular situation arising out of inadequate teaching or course provision.
- ✔ If the complaint is not dealt with in a reasonable time, with consultation with the students affected and a sensible proposal for ensuring the satisfactory 'delivery' of the course, send copies to the vice-chancellor as well as to the dean and head of department.

5

Failing examinations

Degree-awarding powers

A degree or other qualification can be awarded by a university only because it is 'recognized' as a 'degree-giving institution'. It is not illegal to set up as a college and give 'qualifications' in return for very little expenditure of effort, but such spurious 'degrees' are likely to have no 'value' because employers are likely to be aware that they have not come from a 'real' university. The word 'degree' is protected by law.

The question 'what is a real university?' has controversial aspects. Institutions have sometimes laid claim to the 'university' title when they were not themselves recognized degree-awarding institutions. Sometimes students find themselves studying for a degree of a given university at a college that is not itself a university or part of the university in question, but is authorized to award that university's degrees. For example, an institute of Higher Education such as Southampton Institute awards the degrees of Nottingham Trent University, so that a 'Southampton Institute' graduate is actually a graduate of Nottingham Trent. That may be a perfectly acceptable arrangement so long as no one is under any misapprehension about it. It is one of the ways in which a college in the higher education sector can establish its credentials on the way to becoming a university in its own right. However, students may not have had the relationship properly explained to them.

There are two common problems. One is the failure of the university to keep a sufficiently careful eye on the conduct of the process that is leading to the award of its degrees by proxy. The other is the temptation to which a college that is not a university has sometimes succumbed to 'sell' itself as a degree-giving institution in the race to attract overseas students and their large fees.

But if something goes wrong the question arises of who ought to be sued if the university or the franchisee fails to provide the promised programme of study. The answer may depend on which institution has accepted the fees. The institution that actually provides the course will process the application and offer a place subject to acceptance. Once the place is accepted, the franchisee normally accepts the fee. The franchising university stands at arm's length. Where the franchisee is overseas the student may have great difficulty in bringing a case. If in doubt both institutions ought probably to be sued.

Some students attended courses at a college of further education but the degree awarding body was a university. The college was sued and it tried to argue in its defence that there was no contractual relationship between the students and the college. The court accepted that the contractual relationship was between the college and the student.

In another case, an overseas student was accepted by a college to do a master of business administration degree for which the college was a franchisee of an 'old' university. He went to the college and began work. Several months later he was informed that although the college had accepted him, he had not been accepted by the university and that he would have to take an aptitude test. He was told that he could not continue to study. He was therefore unable to take the examinations for which he had been preparing in September. His financial loss was considerable because he had had the expense of moving to England, he had paid fees, and there had been inconvenience, loss of opportunity, loss of employment prospects, distress, embarrassment and damage. He had to find an alternative course, whose fees proved to be much more expensive, and he was not able to transfer credit for the work that he had already done. This student sued only the college, although it might have been wise for him to sue both the college and the university because the university had not ensured that its franchisee was administering its course properly.

Another student on such a course was in an even more curious position. He was a British citizen who had been offered a place on the course. The principal of the college offered him a special arrangement in the form of commission to defray his own fees of £4,750. He was to go to Pakistan as an agent to attract students to the college and if he did not succeed in persuading enough students to come he would pay the balance of the fees he had not 'earned'. He fell into the same trap about the acceptability to the university of his qualifications from Pakistan as the first student (and other students in the same position on the course). In his case there was the further complicating factor of the oral agreement with the Principal on which he had relied.

We do not need to think in terms of things going so far to stress that a student should not be in the dark about the institution to which any complaint ought to be addressed and, again, it is important for students to be told clearly whose degree they are working for and what is the relationship of any validating body to the college in which they are actually studying. Students ought to be able to receive a straight answer to the question of whose degree they are working for and how the degree-awarding institution is supervising the process.

The requirement to pass an examination

A degree is awarded after the student 'passes' the required 'examinations'. For undergraduates, these may take the form of assessed coursework or traditional examinations taken at stages during the course, or at the end of the course, or a combination of the two. In the case of a PhD the examination is usually of a thesis prepared over three or more years, although it is now becoming possible to study for a 'taught doctorate', along the lines of other 'taught' postgraduate courses, such as Master's courses.

However the examination is conducted, students have to 'satisfy' the examiners. That can be where problems begin because students may believe that they have done that and the examiners may maintain that they have not.

Complaining beforehand

Most universities have a requirement that a student must make any complaint about supervision (or any aspect of provision) before taking the examination, that it is not acceptable to say afterwards that the reason for failure was that the university had not provided the necessary teaching or support.

Universities do sometimes have a provision in their regulations to allow some leeway here. In a case of 1999 it emerged that South Bank University had the rule that if a candidate:

> can establish to the satisfaction of the Appeals committee that their performance in the examination was adversely affected by illness or other extenuating circumstances which he or she was unable or for valid reasons unwilling to divulge prior to the Examination Board reaching a decision

the candidate may have grounds for appeal. But a university is extremely unlikely to allow the use of such a clause, and it would be unwise to rely on its being helpful after the event. In one recent case, a student who had lost time preparing for the examination because he had had to help his family cope with a father with a serious progressive illness which sometimes made him violent and dangerous, and which the student had naturally not wanted to talk about, was not allowed the benefit of such a clause.

Don Staniford was working for a PhD at the University of East Anglia's School of Environmental Sciences from 1993. As soon as the University had a complaints procedure, which was not until October 1996, he complained that he had been denied adequate support and supervision. In Don Staniford's case, the University upheld the student's complaint that the supervisor fell below the standard expected for the PhD.

It may not be easy to get a complaint about inadequate supervision 'heard'. A student appealing against the rejection of his PhD thesis pointed out that it had been very difficult for him to complain when he had been asked in front of his supervisor if he was satisfied with the supervision he was receiving.

The same principle of having the allegation lodged in advance applies to giving notice of any special difficulties before taking the examination (such as a problem with arthritis making it difficult to write, so that extra time can be allowed, or dyslexia so severe that the examination papers need to be retyped with corrections to make them intelligible to the examiner). A student may not be keen to discuss difficulties that make him feel 'different' or conspicuous.

These general principles become harder to apply when part of the examination consists of coursework or a dissertation, because it may not be easy to say when the 'examination' begins. Assessed essays may have to be in by a certain date, but one student explained that it took her six times as long as a non-dyslexic student to compose the same amount of prose. So she was able to ask for deferral.

Failing examinations at interim stages

A group of recent cases has involved situations where a university has 'failed' students who have not come to the end of their courses, or who have not even taken a preliminary part of the examination formally.

This is not a new problem. In a case of 30 years ago,[1] the issue was whether students had a right to a hearing, before being finally withdrawn from a course in which they had failed an examination for the second time. It was alleged that the examiners had considered factors that were extraneous to the examination result in making their decisions. An important test case was *Oakes v Sidney Sussex College, Cambridge* [1988] 1 All ER 1004. A student who had been a scholar of the college, one of its stars, was sent down at the end of his second year because of his poor performance in an examination, and not allowed to complete his degree.[2]

Some universities make special provision for appeal against decisions that have been made on the basis of examinations taken part way through a course. In the Progress Committee regulations for the School of Medicine and Dentistry, Queen Mary and Westfield College, London, there has been provision for the exercise of discretion as to whether a candidate could resit the examination, or repeat the year, or would have to withdraw altogether.[3] The rules stipulated that 'the Committee will not require students to withdraw from the College, or debar them from further examination or assessment, without giving them the opportunity to make representations' at a hearing. This establishes the important principle of allowing both sides of the case to be heard. The grounds allowed to be considered in this way are the standard procedural ones that there were circumstances that the examiners did not know about that had led to the poor performance;[4] or that there had been a procedural flaw substantive enough to have affected the outcome.

---

1 *R v Aston University Senate, ex parte Roffey* [1969] 2 QB 538.

2 This case could not be tested fully in the courts, because it ran up against the 'exclusivity of visitorial jurisdiction', but the court felt able to make a number of useful observations before handing the matter back to the college visitor.

3 A progress committee had authority delegated to it to make a decision in each case.

4 Unless the student had simply failed to mention them before the examiners met, when he or she could easily have done so.

If there is a provision for the student to be removed from the course before he has come to the end of it, the university has a duty to conduct the process of doing so with as much care as it gives to the final examination.

Appealing against failure in an examination or against the grade awarded

A student who wants to appeal against an examination result has to begin by clarifying the objection. That means, first, going back to any complaints made before the examination to establish whether they were heard and acted on. It cannot be overemphasized that it is important to raise any *complaint* about supervision or failure to provide the course as advertised or to provide adequate facilities in advance of taking the examination.[5]

A student appealing will have to show that there was a procedural flaw, such as failure to follow the rules laid down for the conduct of the examination. That could include prejudice against the candidate on the part of the examiners, but it should be noted that the 'appearance of bias' is easier to establish than actual bias, for which the threshold is likely to be high. An appeal alleging that the examiner did not like the student is not likely to succeed. There are, however, some areas in which students can reasonably complain. The University of London requires PhD examiners to inform the Academic Registrar about any connections with a candidate or the candidate's supervisor that might make the examiner 'inappropriate' (by prejudicing him or her for or against the candidate). An examiner ought not to have 'played a significant part in advising the candidate' or published joint papers with him.

It will not be possible to appeal on the grounds that the examiners simply got it wrong and the student deserved a higher mark. This is particularly difficult to address because on the face of it the student is less likely to know how well he has performed than those qualified to assess him. The courts take the view that they cannot interfere with expert judgements. An examination result is held to be a matter of 'academic judgement' and

5 See p 104.

unless it is grotesquely wrong and therefore obviously completely unreasonable, no appeal body and no court will interfere with it.

It may, however, be possible to argue that the academic judgement was not really a purely academic judgement at all, because it was contaminated by other factors, or by 'irrelevant considerations'. This covers things like not taking all the relevant factors into consideration or the examiners failing to direct their minds to the right question in assessing their marks.

For example, in Manchester University's appeals procedure for research degrees, appeal might be made 'on grounds alleging':

- that there exist or existed exceptional circumstances affecting the candidate's performance of which the examiners had not been made aware when their decision was taken;
- that there were procedural irregularities in the conduct of the examination;
- that there is evidence of prejudice or bias or of inadequate assessment on the part of one or more of the examiners.

So here, too, the task is to distinguish between 'procedural' flaws and the contention that the examiners simply got their judgement wrong – an argument that the appeal committee would not consider.

There are problems on the borderline here. The leading case on student dissatisfaction with the assessment of work is *R v Visitor to the University of London, ex parte Vijatatunga* [1990] 2 QB 444, [1989] 3 WLR 13. In this case it was held that the selection of examiners was itself a matter of academic judgement and that the visitor could not interfere with it, so again it was not possible to test the point very far. The tendency of the courts is undoubtedly to err respectfully on the side of not interfering with anything that might in any way seem a matter of academic judgement. Yet the modern London University regulations about PhD examiners might put an appellant in a different position because the university is bound by the rules it set itself.

This is territory on which it is important to particularize the grounds of appeal very carefully. It is a technical job, requiring skill and experience. The student should be able to expect independent experienced help and should ask for it. Yet the reality is that universities often do not provide a student appellant with the expert assistance he or she needs to draw up an appeal. They may even be so unclear about the grounds they will accept that they cannot give the appellant a list. That is a proper ground for complaint in itself, and the student should not be rushed into submitting a statement of the grounds for appeal without proper preparation, because an appeal can normally be conducted only once.

Some universities will allow for re-appeal, if fresh evidence comes to light. On the other hand, there are usually time limits for appeals and students should be careful not to put an appeal in late. If a deadline is missed, the university can stand on its procedures and refuse to hear the appeal at all.

Procedural grounds

A student seeking to appeal should ask for a copy of the procedural rules the examiners followed. Did they keep their own rules?

On the question whether the examiners have failed to follow the proper procedure, various practical questions may be asked, to put flesh on the bones. Did the examiners actually read all the scripts? Was the external examiner present for the examiners' meeting? Did someone add the marks up wrongly?

The student may succeed in an appeal if he can obtain details of his scripts, and the marks given for individual questions, and examiners' comments. His rights to see these are often a matter of dispute, but the trend is to allow it and the courts may support that. Students are likely to have an uphill struggle to get this information, but they may have a right to it, in the interests of what the courts call 'the fair disposal of the case'. They may also now (or at the latest by autumn 2001) have a right to it under the Data Protection Act 1998. In other words, unless the student knows enough about what happened to be able to ask the right questions, the appeal cannot be run fairly. This is a matter of natural justice.

That there was some procedural irregularity in the conduct of the examination is likely to be the best ground on which to succeed. Leaving out relevant considerations is an accepted error of procedure, because something has been omitted that ought to have been taken into account. But it is also connected with the forming of the judgement, because the 'leaving out' may have been psychological rather than a matter of not taking facts or information into the examination meeting.

> A mark...awarded at an examiners' meeting where irrelevant and damaging personal factors have been allowed to enter into the evaluation of a candidate's written paper is something more than an informed exercise of an academic judgement. Where evidence shows that something extraneous has entered into the process of academic judgement, one of two results may follow depending on the nature of the fault: either the decision will fall...or the court may require reasons to be given, so that the decision can either be seen to be sound or can be seen or (absent reasons) be inferred to be flawed.[6]

Another kind of procedural irregularity consists in breach by the examiners of the university's own rules. It is important, for that reason, to be sure what the examiners were required to do. The university ought to be able to give the student a set of the regulations under which the examiners were required to work, but it is rare for that to happen. For example, if each paper was marked by two examiners, did the first one give the second one his marks before the second one looked at the papers? Was this allowed under the rules? Examiners are often guilty of this sort of lapse.

In November 1998 a student appealed against a decision of an Examination Board to award a Diploma of Higher Education at level 3 (instead of the BA (Hons)) on the grounds that there had been 'a material and significant administrative error' in the recording and communication of results. The appeal was upheld, although there followed some difficulty in determining what was to be done about the outstanding missing credits that the student needed to make up in order to be eligible for the degree. Here something had gone administratively wrong, so there was a clear 'procedural error'.

If it is found that there has been procedural irregularity the examination may be deemed never to have taken place, and it has to be conducted again. But even here the student is not home and dry. There is frequently a provision in the rules under which they may appeal that says that even if a procedural flaw is discovered, it may be decided that it made no difference to the outcome. There is a duty to *show* why that is the case.[7] But universities

---

6 *R v Universities Funding Council, ex parte Institute of Dental Surgery* [1994] 1 All ER 651. Cf: *R v Privy Council, ex parte Vijagatunga* [1988] 1 QB 322; *Salek v University of Dundee* (1992), *The Times*, 23 December; *Carlton v Glasgow Caledonian University* (1993) (OH) unreported.

7 *R v Board of Governors of Sheffield Hallam University and others, ex parte R* [1995] ELR 267.

easily get away with not doing so, merely making an 'assertion' that they proceeded correctly.

Academic judgement

The second heading under which a student is likely to want to overturn a decision is that the decision itself was wrong. This takes us into the area of 'academic judgement'. This is extremely difficult to overturn, and the courts will almost never intervene to challenge it. In *R v University of Portsmouth, ex parte Lakareber* [1999] ELR 135 CA at 140 it was held that 'only the clearest and most obvious unfairness or departure from the university's own regulations would justify an attempt by judicial review to impugn an academic decision of this character'. It is important to keep this clearly in mind.

That is as true for the assessment of the publications of academic staff in the Research Assessment Exercise as for the assessment of the work of students in examinations:

> Peer review...is suspect enough to anyone who knows how much bitchiness and trendiness there is in academic life. But at least the submitted publications would surely be evidence on which judgements of a sort could be made. So it might be if each was carefully read by at least two panel members. But what happened? Panels with small numbers of submissions were able to ensure that the *majority* of cited publications were read by at least *one panel member*...But what if the numbers of submissions were large. Here the whole system imploded...Reading of publications was abandoned as 'not practicable' and 'more weight had to be given to the vehicle for the publication'...Some journals were rated more highly than others'.[8]

In *M v London Guildhall University* [1998] ELR 149 CA a law student was not given his degree. He brought an action in negligence, breach of contract and misrepresentation. In response, London Guildhall University offered him a degree. He continued with the proceeding because he wanted an *honours* degree, but there he went too far because he was asking the courts to make an academic judgement to substitute for that of the University. Again in *R v*

---

8 John Griffith, *Times Higher Education Supplement*, 8 April 1994.

Leeds Metropolitan University, ex parte Manders [1998] ELR 502 there was an attempt to seek review of the decision of a board of examiners.

The difficulty is that the academics who make the judgement are considered to be experts, and the courts recognize that they are not expert in physics, literature, theology, chemistry, but only in the application of the law. So a student who is saying 'my work is better than that, I deserved a higher mark' is not going to be able to get his or her results reviewed. There are changes afoot in respect of decision-making by other kinds of professionals. If questions are not asked (and pressed) about what is 'fair' in forming this sort of judgement, the situation will not improve.

It is arguable that universities should be vicariously[9] liable for the acts or omissions of their employees. In a university academic staff have a duty as employees and also as professionals to provide a standard of teaching, which, if they act as examiners, also includes an obligation to exercise a professional level of academic judgement. That may suggest an avenue of recourse for students who seek to challenge an examination result. If there is evidence of failure to maintain proper professional standards of academic judgement there may be a case against the university or college.

Reconciling conflicting opinions

An especially difficult area in the field of challenging academic judgements is where there has been a disagreement among those who formed the judgement. That could be the case with examiners' marks, where the same paper is double marked and the examiners do not agree. There is then a duty to talk through the reasons for giving the different marks. The possibility of doing that will depend on the examiners who marked the papers all being present, or having written out their reasons in full for the other examiners to see. The *Times Higher Education Supplement* of 16 July 1999 carried an article on the unsatisfactoriness of external examiners not being present, but the same principle may apply if any of those who *awarded* marks do not join in the task of deciding the final marks.

---

9 The decision in *X (Minors) v Bedfordshire County Council* [1995] 2 AC 633 was restrictively interpreted in *Phelps v Hillingdon London Borough Council* [1999] 1 All ER 421 and see Hedley, 'Negligence – diagnosis of dyslexia' [1999] CLJ 270. Here it was held that an educational psychologist was primarily employed to advise the school and the local authority and had not assumed a personal responsibility to the plaintiff. But that exclusion does not apply to teachers, who arguably have a direct duty to those they teach to take reasonable professional care.

A student took an MMus at an old university in 1994–95. He and the only other student doing composition as part of the degree were both given a three-month extension until December 1996. There was a five-month delay in obtaining marks from the external examiner. When they became available they overruled all the internal marks and the student had do redo some of the work. He was not able to obtain access to supervision until October 1996, 10 months after the examination.

The work was redone and resubmitted and again passed internally and failed externally. The department accepted the external examiner's marks and in letters and a meeting during the summer of 1996 it also accepted that, as he put it to the vice-chancellor, 'the University had some responsibility for my predicament'. There was some difficulty in obtaining replies to letters during September and October 1996.

When he tried to complain, he reported that the professor of music had responded in a telephone conversation 'do you want me to ask the board to withdraw its approval for the award of the diploma?' He took this as a threat. This kind of threat is not uncommon. A student should never be asked to withdraw a complaint as a condition of being allowed to continue with the course.

This student wrote to the vice-chancellor on legal advice to ask for compensation. In a letter of 28 August 1997, he complained of 'huge, outrageous, continuing delays, inadequate advice, and the constant conflicts of academic judgement relating to this matter, which have resulted in the loss of two extra years of my life'. In December 1997 the university agreed to refund all the course fees. In the following academic year he completed an MA in music at another university, without difficulty, the external examiner this time agreeing with the internal marks.

This student's complaint included the allegation that he was not given adequate tuition (the same discrepancy between internal and external marks occurred in the case of the other student on the course with him in 1994–95) and that there had been administrative failings. The core of his difficulty, however, was that there was no mechanism for resolving contradictory academic judgements and deciding which was right.

Giving of references

A promising area here is the development of case law on the giving of references. An examiner's judgement has a certain amount in common with a reference. It is a value judgement of a person's performance, which will affect the individual's employment prospects for the future. Michele Brenton won a landmark case reported in *The Times* in May 1996 against the former Polytechnic of Wales, now Glamorgan University. She had been due to start work with Monmouth Borough Council within three days when the job offer was withdrawn. The council said that her reference was unsatisfactory but it would not let her see the document. It took her years and a great deal of litigation to obtain the reference. When she was finally able to read it she found that it questioned her 'personal attitude and emotional state' and said that her work as a student was of a very low standard. (No allowance appears to have been made for the fact that she was coping with the stress of a divorce during her last year at Glamorgan.) She accepted an out-of-court settlement for the loss of earnings in the job she lost as a consequence of this reference.

This kind of secret criticism, to which the 'accused' has no opportunity to reply, is likely gradually to be outlawed by new Data Protection legislation and by the incorporation in the United Kingdom of human rights legislation. In the meantime a student can only try to insist on seeing what is said about him or her so as to establish whether the university has exercised due care in the 'preparation' of what has been said by examiners or lecturers.

The leading case here is *Spring v Guardian Assurance* [1994] IRLR 460 HL. An employer provided a reference to a prospective new employer without taking proper precautions to ensure that the information was accurate in the light of the information available to the employer at that time. The employer owes a duty of care to the employee to take reasonable steps to verify the information on which the reference is based. The obligation is only to state an honestly held belief, but the belief must be based on facts whose correctness has been properly checked. The same principles would apply in the case of an examination report or a reference for a student.

Delay

Delay is a problem in its own right. It may amount to maladministration,[10] but knowing that is not of much consolation to a student faced with a wait of weeks or months for the answer to a question that, to him or her, is very urgent. The *Times Higher Education Supplement* of 12 July 1996 noted that a visitor case at Birmingham University had lasted eight years, and it is common for a student still to be involved in a dispute ten years after it began.

The student himself may be guilty of delay. Delay may be a ground for seeking to question an examination outcome, but that can go either way. In *R v University of Central England, ex parte Iqbal Sandhu* [1999] ELR 121, Iqbal Sandhu had submitted his dissertation late. The case turned partly on whether an extension had been granted. (It is important to seek extensions in good time and to establish clearly whether they *have* been allowed and for how long.) In the event, he was deemed to have submitted late and no marks were awarded for the dissertation. It was then argued on his behalf that that was a disproportionate penalty. This case is an awful warning because the court decided that the university had given notice that that would be the result of late submission. That was 'what [the university] had said in their rules they would do and they did in fact do it'.[11]

In *R v Visitor to the University of Wales, ex parte Liam Sweeney,* Liam Sweeney was an MPhil student at University College, Cardiff, enrolled at the College's School of European studies, who complained that there was an inordinate delay in conducting a *viva voce* examination on his thesis (a substantial piece of work of 60,000 words) and that there was then more delay in supplying him with the examiners' report, so that he could not properly lodge an appeal. Would the inordinate delay cause some prejudice? It is difficult to defend a piece of work 13 months after submission.

In May 1998 Stuart Morris was told that his PhD thesis was to be awarded only the MPhil degree (by Manchester University). The result of the examination was not given to him until 15 months after he had submitted the thesis. He appealed on the grounds of procedural irregularity and prejudice or inadequate assessment. He alleged that his examiners did not

10 Hinds, W, 'Ombudsman Reports', *Education and the Law*, 10 (1998) 81.
11 *R v University of Central England, ex parte Iqbal Sandhu* [1999] ELR 121 at 134.

possess the relevant expertise. He said that not all relevant considerations had been taken into account in that some important aspects of the dissertation were ignored by the examiners. He said that the criteria laid down in the PhD regulations had not been followed. Most important, for our purposes, he said that 14 months was an unreasonable time to have to wait for a *viva*. It would not have been fixed even then if he had not brought pressure to bear for an explanation of the delay (which he was not given). He said he could not perform as well after so long an interval as he might have done if the *viva* had been held when what he had written in his thesis was still fresh in his mind.

Giving reasons

It can be difficult to get any decision reviewed unless reasons have been given, because the student who wants to challenge the outcome may not have enough information to enable him to point to a flaw in the way the decision was reached. There has hitherto been no general duty to give reasons for administrative decisions in English law,[12] but the trend is towards requiring them in more and more situations. It is now good practice to give reasons and universities can no longer expect to get away with not doing so. Many of the cases touched on in this book dragged on and on and became extremely expensive and damaging for the institution because it would not explain itself to the student when a problem first arose. It is much easier to come clean at once and hold an open discussion of what has happened than to resist disclosure or explanation until the problem has swollen out of all proportion and the student's career prospects may be irretrievably damaged by the institution's delay and intransigence.

Some of the recent cases demonstrate the trend towards change; the requirement to give reasons where someone is aggrieved by a decision made by a public body is based on sheer reasonableness (for which the threshold is high) or on fairness (under rules of fairness and natural justice). The argument is stronger in cases where the aggrieved person's future career or livelihood is at stake, as is often the case for students. In

12 One of the foundation cases here is *R v Civil Service Appeal Board, ex parte Cunningham* [1991] 4 All ER 310 CA.

such circumstances, the courts are increasingly adopting the view that if no reasons are given this will raise doubts, and they will often intervene to end doubt and refuse to give the decision maker the 'benefit of the doubt'.

An example is *R v Lambeth Borough Council, ex parte Walters* (1993) *The Times*, 6 October DC. Ms Walters was homeless. She was offered housing, which she said was unsuitable for her four-year-old, who had spina bifida. She appealed. The council rejected the appeal but gave no reasons. Ms Walters was successful in a judicial review application. It was held that it was unfair of the council not to provide details of its medical assessment and adequate reasons for its decision. It was even suggested that English law was reaching a point where there *was* a general duty to give reasons. In another case, *R v Secretary of State for Education, ex parte Standish* (1993) *The Times* 15 November DC, the minister failed to give reasons for his decisions debarring a teacher from employment. Because there were no reasons the court was prepared to infer the irrationality of the decision. The Human Rights Act may now require the giving of reasons.

Student action checklist

- ✔ Ask the university to explain what counts as 'part of the examination'. This can be very important if there is to be an appeal. Are assessed essays done during the course 'part' of the examination? Is a *viva voce* examination 'part' of the examination? Is a decision whether to allow a MPhil student to go on to a PhD 'part' of the MPhil examination?
- ✔ Make any complaint about the provision of teaching or the facilities or the 'delivery' of the course in good time and, in any case, before taking the examination.
- ✔ Send in details of any medical condition affecting performance or requiring special facilities in good time before taking the examination, with medical certificates if necessary.
- ✔ If there is to be an appeal, ask for full reasons and sight of all the documents on which the examiners wrote anything, and for the procedural rules under which the examiners worked. Ask for the minutes of examiners' meetings, so that you can see whether the procedural rules were followed.

6

Keeping the rules

Fair procedures

The conduct of appeals about examination results is only one of the areas where rules of fairness are required and we must turn next to that wider arena. Here the Human Rights Act 1998 will be important.[1] This incorporates the articles of the European Convention on Human Rights, except for Article 13, into English law from October 2000 (earlier in Scottish law). That means that a student will be able to go directly to the courts in this country and will not have to take the much longer, slower and more expensive route through the European courts.

A starting point for universities, and an urgent one, is to review their procedures to ensure that they comply with the requirements of the Human Rights Act, to make a policy decision about the degree of detail and explicitness they are to contain and to make sure that students are given copies of all procedures affecting them, together with explanatory material.

A university that faces a considerable task here is Cambridge. One of the last universities to tackle the need to create a student complaints code, it nevertheless has in its Statutes and Ordinances several sets of 'rules of procedure' to be used for *disciplinary* purposes. Its rules of procedure for the University Tribunal[2] say that the parties to a hearing are the person charged

---

1 Anthony Bradley, The implications of the Human Rights Act 1998 for schools, unpublished paper dated 9 June 2000. See pp 141–42.

2 Cambridge University (1999) *Statutes and Ordinances of the University of Cambridge*, Cambridge University Press, Cambridge, p 197.

with a disciplinary offence; the University Advocate (who presents the case for the university against the person charged) and any other party added by the Tribunal or 'of their own motion', that is at the party's own wish. There is a right to representation, a right to not less than 14 days' notice of the hearing, with procedural information and a copy of the charge or charges. If new documentary evidence is produced at any stage, the person charged is to be allowed an adjournment sufficient to enable him or her to consider the additional evidence and respond to it, and to introduce further evidence as appropriate. There is a right to an oral hearing and the hearing may be in public unless the person charged requests that it be held *in camera*. The standard of proof is set at the criminal standard of 'reasonable doubt'. There is, however, a provision for hearing a case in the absence of the person entitled to be present 'if in the opinion of the Chairman such exclusion is necessary for the maintenance of order'. That might fall foul of the Human Rights Act, Article 6, but the remainder of the provision is reasonably adequate.

Yet this Tribunal is for hearing discipline cases against members of staff. The University Court, which hears disciplinary charges against students, has much less elaborate protections. There is nothing in its procedures *requiring* the student charged to be given the right to representation, no right to at least 14 days' notice of the hearing, with procedural information and a copy of the charge or charges. There is no repetition of the protection for staff that if new documentary evidence is produced at any stage, the person charged is to be allowed an adjournment sufficient to enable him or her to consider the additional evidence and respond to it, and to introduce further evidence as appropriate.[3] On the other hand, the Summary Court, which also tries students for certain types of alleged offence, does require some of these protections.[4] This kind of confusion can arise when procedures are created piecemeal and without systematic review of their relationship to one another. There is no excuse for universities not to overhaul their procedures to ensure that they are internally consistent. They will have an opportunity to do this in ensuring that their procedures are Human Rights Act compliant.

3 Cambridge University (1999) *Statutes and Ordinances of the University of Cambridge*, Cambridge University Press, Cambridge, p 200.

4 Cambridge University (1999) *Statutes and Ordinances of the University of Cambridge*, Cambridge University Press, Cambridge, p 200–01.

There is also no excuse for universities not to give 'preventive' training in procedural fairness to everyone who is to take part in appeals, disciplinary or complaints hearings. The more staff who are familiar with such rules the less likely it is that disputes will escalate and become expensive and intractable.[5] The rules that make a procedure 'fair' are not exactly the same for all kinds of decision making. It depends on the seriousness of the matter for the person concerned and the kind of issue under consideration. For example, a disciplinary procedure that may lead to the expulsion of a student has to be more rigorous in certain respects than a procedure for taking administrative decisions. Appeals procedures have to be sufficiently rigorous to test the fairness of procedures 'below' them, whose outcomes have been appealed against.

From the student's point of view, the three types of procedure in which he is most likely to become involved are 'disciplinary', 'complaint' and 'appeal' procedures.

The main rules of fairness

At the bottom of all fair[6] procedures are two principles, known as the 'rules of natural justice'. This is a highly technical area, but the basic ideas are quite straightforward.

The *nemo iudex* rule says that no one may be judge in his own case. This is the 'bias' rule. That means that any kind of conflict of interest ought to be declared and someone who may be prejudiced, or even appear to be prejudiced, ought not to be allowed to take part in the decision making.

The *audi alteram partem* rule says that both sides of the case should be heard. Under this rule come the requirements that no one may be tried in his absence, or without being given notice of the charge against him and proper time to prepare his defence, with a chance to examine any witnesses and to see the evidence brought against him.[7] There is no absolute right to a hearing except in discipline cases, but a university probably ought to allow one if it is requested.

5 See references in Palfreyman, D (1999) The HEI-student legal relationship, with special reference to the USA experience, *Education and the Law*, **11**, 5–24, at pp 6–7.

6 The Dearing Report's recommendations 25 and 60 are relevant.

7 The denial of any rights of disclosure of documentation can be a serious obstacle to a student receiving a fair hearing, although the new Data Protection Act (1988) may make a helpful difference. Article 6 of the Human Rights Act 1988 reinforces the rule on fairness.

These rules were developed from at least the late Roman period, to protect the accused in criminal or disciplinary cases. It is only very recently that they have come to be accepted good practice in administrative decision making as well as in a 'quasi-judicial' arena. It still seems to be true that those who are already members of a university have a right to natural justice, whereas candidates for admission do not:[8]

> The context of educational societies involves a special factor which is not present in other contexts, namely the relation of tutor and pupil; that is to say the society is charged with the upbringing and supervision of the pupil under tuition, be the society a university or a college or a school. Where this relationship exists it is quite plain that on the one hand in certain circumstances the body or individual acting on behalf of the society must be regarded as acting in a quasi-judicial capacity – expulsion from the society is the obvious example. On the other hand, there is a wide range of circumstances in which the body or individual is concerned to impose penalties by way of domestic discipline. In these circumstances it seems to me that the body or individual is not acting in a quasi-judicial capacity at all but in a magisterial capacity, i.e. in the performance of the rights and duties vested in the society as to the upbringing and supervision of the members of the society.[9]

In other words, the educational context is special. In the 1960s there was an attempt to distinguish between the 'quasi-judicial' process needed in a case which might lead to the student being expelled, and actions under 'domestic laws'. Things looked different in universities when this was said in 1967. The age of majority was then still 21 and a paternalistic approach still seemed appropriate. Even in this period some were ready to criticize the unwillingness of the courts to call universities to account:

> Once again a case of student discipline has reached the High Court, once again the University authorities have failed to observe the principles of natural justice and once again the student has been sent away without remedy because the court's discretion has been exercised against him.[10]

---

8 Students who sought to challenge the admissions policy of the Bar Council by judicial review on the grounds of unfairness were, however, allowed to proceed. Megarry J in *John v Rees* [1969] 2 WLR 1294 at 1331 and see Hepple BA (1969) Natural justice for rusticated students [1969] CLJ 169.

9 *Durayappah v Fernando* [1967] 2 AC 337.

10 Wade, HWR, Nudism and natural justice (1971) LQR 320 and Hepple, BA, Natural justice for rusticated students (1969) CLJ 169.

Universities can be very vague about the ground rules of fairness. In *R v Board of Governors of Sheffield Hallam University and others, ex parte R* [1995] ELR 267, 'R' was a second year student on a PE teacher-training course. In the second year 'R' had to give evidence at a disciplinary hearing against fellow-students. She said that as a result she had been bullied and beaten up. She was suspended with some others in a drug-taking investigation on 9 February 1993. The regulations stipulated that there must be 'documented proof of adequate prior warning', but that was not available.[11]

This case was handled with a procedural confusion that is common in universities. A hearing was held, but several detailed reports were produced there without warning. The solicitor who had attended as the appellant's 'friend' objected that the appellant had not been given sufficient time to prepare. He was ignored and the academic board made the decision to expel the applicant from her course on the ground of failure 'to adhere to the professional standards specified for training purposes', and that her record should show that she was 'unsuitable to enter the teaching profession'.

The appellant's solicitor appealed on the grounds that there had not been sufficient prior written warning and that there had not been sufficient prior disclosure to enable the applicant to prepare her case. A panel of three members of the governing body dismissed this appeal.

The judge said at the judicial review stage, 'She was in my judgement entitled to a clear statement not only of what she ought to do, but linked with it, of the possible consequences of her not doing it.'[12] When this came to court, the judge, commenting on the breach of the rule about 'hearing the other side' said, 'A student who stood at risk of expulsion should have had adequate notice of the substance of what was to be alleged against her.'[13] He pointed out that 'if a party in breach of proper procedure is to escape the ordinary consequence by asserting that nothing has been lost by the breach, it is for the party to demonstrate it'.[14]

The rule about conflict of interest can be sidestepped, too. It can often be a problem that the same members of the senior academic and administrative staff of the university act as accuser, prosecutor, judge and jury (for

11 *R v Board of Governors of Sheffield Hallam University and others, ex parte R* [1995] ELR 267 at 282.
12 *R v Board of Governors of Sheffield Hallam University and others, ex parte R* [1995] ELR 267 at 282.
13 *R v Board of Governors of Sheffield Hallam University and others, ex parte R* [1995] ELR 267 at 286.
14 *R v Board of Governors of Sheffield Hallam University and others, ex parte R* [1995] ELR 267.

example, the Oxford Proctors). Universities ought to make provision for the student accused of an offence to have a student member of the panel or judicial body that 'sits' on his case. The problem here is the danger of bias we have already touched on. In the Sheffield Hallam case the judgment spoke of 'a real possibility of "infection" of the decision...a competent Chairperson who has formed a view as to the right outcome will generally steer his or her colleagues unobtrusively towards that outcome'.[15]

In *Rajah v Royal College of Surgeons in Ireland* [1994] 1 IRLM 232, the applicant was a medical student who challenged her college's decision not to let her resit her third year examinations for a second time. Rajah said that when she appealed, one of the members of the appeal board had belittled and intimidated her and so she had not felt able to raise certain personal matters in mitigation. When she applied for judicial review she argued that she had not had a fair hearing, that she had been given no reasons for the decision and that the college had not told her about the procedures. The court rejected her application partly on jurisdictional grounds, but also because the judge did not consider that these flaws amounted to the denial of a fair hearing. The courts have therefore demonstrated that there must be clear and good grounds for the claim of 'denial of a fair hearing' to succeed.[16]

The right to be treated according to the rules of natural justice can be overridden by 'necessity'. If there is only one body which can consider a matter, it will have to be allowed to do so, even though it may be sitting in judgement on its own former decision. A student at Liverpool John Moores University on a pharmacy course had problems at the end of her second year. She failed her exams and was not allowed to go on to her final year. She challenged this decision and the University accepted that 'serious errors had been made in dealing with her'. But when she objected to the same Academic Board reconsidering the case on two occasions, it was held that 'since [this] was the only body which could decide ultimately on her eligibility for a degree, such reconsideration was inevitable'.[17] That does not allow a university to have it all its own way, however.

---

15 *R v Board of Governors of Sheffield Hallam University and others, ex parte R* [1995] ELR 267 at 285.

16 On the implications of the implementation of the Human Rights Act 1998 that came into force in October 2000, see pp 75–78 and pp 141–42.

17 *R v Liverpool John Moores University, ex parte Hayes* [1998] ELR 261.

The basics

Stage one

- The university must not identify itself with members of staff complained against. It must merely provide the forum or jurisdiction within which the complaints are to be impartially and independently examined. Nor must it treat an appeal as though it were lodged 'against' the university. Again, the matter must be impartially and independently examined. When the matter is disciplinary, whether the charge is against a member of staff or a student, it becomes appropriate for the university, as the disciplinary authority, to act as a party – but only then.
- One of the implications of this need to be clear-headed about who the parties are, is that the university must not provide free legal help for a member of staff complained against unless it provides the same help for the student.

Stage two

- There must be arrangements to ensure that an impartial person or body considers any matter, whether complaint, disciplinary or appeal, and can be seen to be independent of the administration of the university.
- There should be sufficient notice for everyone before any decision is taken. Any charge or accusation, complaint or appeal must be made in writing and given to everyone involved in good time.
- A preliminary meeting or hearing to discuss procedure is often helpful, and that should not normally take place in the absence of the student concerned.
- The student should put forward a statement of the case, so that the issues are clear and well defined.

Stage three

- In a disciplinary case or where a complaint is against a person, there must normally be a hearing. There is not necessarily a right to a hearing in an appeal about the outcome of an examination.
- If there is to be a hearing, both parties should submit relevant documentation in advance of the hearing. A reasonable minimum period would be seven days, perhaps longer outside term time.
- Time must be allowed for requests for disclosure of documents to be met.
- The principles of natural justice require that all written material and documents to be taken into consideration must be seen by all parties.
- If new information is introduced during the proceedings, the parties should be offered sufficient opportunity to consider it and to comment on it, and that will normally require an adjournment.
- Similarly, if new charges arise, they must be properly set out in writing and given to everyone and the process above should be gone through again for the new charges.
- There must be an opportunity for both sides to examine witnesses.
- The student should not be expected to manage alone. He should be provided with help in framing the appeal and he has in any case a right to a representative of his own choosing (although not necessarily to a lawyer – some universities stipulate that no lawyers should be involved so as to keep things flexible and informal).
- The question of who should go first in presenting arguments depends on the nature of the case, whether it is an appeal by the student or a disciplinary case against the student. At a disciplinary hearing, the case of the university may be put first and the student given the opportunity to ask questions. Then the case for the student should be put and the university side allowed to ask questions. Then there should be a summing up by the university and finally a summing up by the student, who should probably have the last word whether he or she is the complainant or the accused, because the 'weaker' party should always be given that advantage.

- There should be no interruptions except for purposes of clarification.
- At the end of the hearing the appeal body should give a clear indication of the procedure to be followed for the giving of the decision. The decision should be given in writing and it should provide reasons.

Distinguishing disciplinary from academic penalties

The point that it is not acceptable for a university to impose academic penalties for an offence that was not academic (such as not paying bills for accommodation) arises again in a different forum: that of plagiarism. Can a student properly suffer an 'academic' penalty for misconduct that is not academic? That will depend perhaps on the nature of the misconduct. 'Rustication', or 'sending down', used to be common where a student had committed some disciplinary offence, and that of course meant an automatic educational deprivation, yet the offence might have been a sexual misdemeanour.

Plagiarism or cheating is an area where the misconduct is clearly both 'disciplinary' and 'academic', and indeed US courts have had difficulty in deciding whether cheating is an academic or a disciplinary offence (see below).

It is reasonable to argue that any penalty within the law of education should not be disproportionate to the offence. Universities are, first and foremost, providers of education and not disciplinary bodies. Since the recent changes in the contractual basis that has become more important. It may be relevant that a service provider cannot 'discipline' the 'purchaser' of a 'service'. Yet, as we shall see in what follows, universities routinely assume powers to discipline students as 'members of the community' if they disrupt its good order.

Discretion

R v London Borough of Bexley, ex parte Angela Bridget Jones, 29 April 1994, CO 3013/93 was a case about the refusal to grant a discretionary award in the days when fees and maintenance grants were available for certain courses only if the local education authority (LEA) chose to pay them. 'Discretion' is an important concept for students who want to challenge an unfavourable decision, because it allows a person or body with authority a great deal of freedom to decide something.

Certain things are not allowed, however. Discretion is not unlimited. One form of 'abuse of discretion' would be to make a decision so unreasonable that no reasonable person could possibly have arrived at it. Another is to 'fetter' the discretion improperly by imposing rules that prevent its being a real exercise of discretion at all. In the *Jones* case, it was alleged that a rule was being applied so rigidly that it was impossible to allow for the special circumstances presented by individual cases. A policy may be applied too rigidly in examination assessment as in making decisions about discretionary awards.[18] In an appeal procedure there has to be a fair process that ensures that there is provision for exceptional circumstances to be taken into account.[19]

There had at one stage been some intimation that consideration might be given to exceptional cases. That turned out to be important. There had been conflicting messages from the local authority to this prospective student. The LEA first said that it would make an award and then, in July 1993, said that it would not make an award because the policy on awards no longer included her course.[20] The Minutes of the Libraries, Youth and Further Education Sub-Committee of 15 March 1994 said that:

'Exceptional cases falling outside the normal policy will be considered on an individual basis by the Educational Services Secretary, in consultation with…'

---

18 *R v Shropshire County Council, ex parte Jones* [1997] ELR 357 at 368.

19 *R v Shropshire County Council, ex parte Jones* [1997] ELR 357.

20 Leggatt J said in his judgement: 'The principle is well-established and it is common ground that a Local Authority cannot adopt a policy which precludes the exercise of its discretion, nor can it slavishly follow a policy without regard to the merits of individual cases'. Those principles are established by *R v London County Council, ex parte Corrie* [1918] 1 KB 68 per Avory J at 74; *R v Port of London Authority, ex parte Kynoch Ltd* [1919] 1 KB 176; *Stringer v Minister for Housing and Local Government* [1971] WLR 1, 281; [1980] 78 LGR 677.

The judgement says that:

> It is, of course, legitimate for a statutory body such as the Respondents to adopt a policy designed to ensure a rational and consistent approach to the exercise of a statutory discretion in particular types of case. But it can only do so provided that the policy fairly admits of exceptions to it. In my judgement, the Respondents effectually disabled themselves from considering individual cases and there has been no convincing evidence that at any material time they had an exceptions procedure worth the name. There is no indication that there was a genuine willingness to consider individual cases. On the contrary, there is every indication of rigid adherence to their policy...An effective exceptions procedure depends on having the information available by reference to which special circumstances can be assessed, with a view to considering whether an exception should be made in favour of the individual concerned.

Here, it was held, the LEA could not make a rule that did not allow it to take account of the particular circumstances of the case. In another case, the same principle was tested:

> If the only permitted exceptions are those where the circumstances are 'most extraordinary' the authority appears to be very close to instituting a blanket policy which while in theory admitting of exceptions may not, in reality, result in the proper consideration of each individual case on its merits. [21]

Warwickshire County Council adopted a new policy that incorporated criteria for determining 'exceptional circumstances'. That was tested in *R v Warwickshire County Council, ex parte Williams* [1995] ELR 326 at 333 where the position of the courts began to swing the other way. They began to exercise their own discretion in favour of a greater freedom of discretion. Shiemann J held that: 'Local authorities should be free to decide, each according to its own local sense of priorities, how much to spend on discretionary awards including a freedom to decide to spend very little indeed if anything'.[22]

---

21 *R v Warwickshire County Council, ex parte Collymore* [1995] ELR 217 at 227.

22 In *R v Southwark London Borough Council, ex parte Udu, The Times,* 30 October 1995 CA there was a similar decision that the courts would not intervene in the discretion of LEAs to make decisions about discretionary awards. Udu was a law graduate seeking a discretionary award to enable him to attend the legal practice course.

There followed *R v Buckinghamshire County Council, ex parte Pawan Sharma* and *R v Wiltshire County Council, ex parte Lakhbir Kaur,* which were heard as a single case. In the judgement there was reference to 'the conflict between the need for consistency and the need to meet the circumstances of individual cases'. In these cases it was held at the time that it was not unlawful for the local authority to define the meaning of exceptional circumstances. It had been argued that without definition there would be inconsistency and that that was contrary to good public administration. But it was decided that, to define 'exceptional circumstances' would have the disadvantage that some categories might be admitted, since no list was likely to be exhaustive.

There it rested, and the particular question of discretionary *awards* partly died away because of the ending of the old system of funding for students. But these basic rules about the exercise of discretion apply in other areas where a university may do something 'discretionary'.

Just as decision-making must be reasonable, so it is not permitted to be random. Before a decision is taken there has to be a policy or rules for determining the outcome. In *R v London Borough of Ealing, ex parte Matharu and another*, 3 May 1995, the judge granted leave to apply for judicial review where the relief sought was for a mandatory order (an instruction from the court)[23] for the respondent to adopt a policy setting out the *principles* of eligibility for an appeal for a discretionary grant.

For universities the important lesson is that these basic rules ought to be in everyone's minds when committees take decisions affecting students, whatever types of decision they are. It also demonstrates the need for openness and clarity in the process of decision-making.

Student discipline

How does a university get its rules? Usually it makes them itself, though it may have a few imposed on it by law, as happened under the Education Reform Act of 1988. In many cases, a university's laws have to be approved by the Privy Council, as do those that govern Oxford and Cambridge and their colleges, and those of most 'old' universities. There are special rules in

23 See pp 139–41.

the Further and Higher Education Act 1992 determining the laws of the universities set up by that Act. 'Subordinate' rules do not all have to be formally approved in that way, but they do have to be in conformity with the main rules. A university cannot do what it likes.

For students it is likely to be the lower-level laws, the subordinate rules, which matter, for they will tend to be embodied in the codes of practice which affect students most directly. The main rule affecting 'subordinate legislation' made internally by universities is that it must not be in conflict with the higher level rules under which it is made. For example, a university is a place of 'education, learning and research', and the statutes of a pre-1992 university frequently contain the statement that that is its purpose. So it could not make a regulation saying that education cannot take place on the premises.

A second general rule is that the regulation must be made by someone who has been given authority to make it. So a rule or regulation would have no force unless powers to make it had been properly delegated under the university's procedures.

Every university ought to have a discipline code that is published and made available to all students when they are registered. In most universities the provisions made for disciplining students are more comprehensive and fully worked out than the provisions for students to make complaints.

The code should be clear about the activities or actions that are offences against the code and about what will happen if the student breaks the code.

It should be fair. That means, in accordance with the rules of natural justice we have just been examining:

- it should provide for students to be given full details of any accusation against them and any documents upon which the university is going to rely;
- it should give time for the defence to be prepared;
- the student should be told who will 'try' his or her case and be allowed to object if he or she has a good reason to believe anyone will not be independent in forming a judgement;
- there should be a hearing;
- the student should be allowed to be accompanied by a representative or friend (although sometimes a solicitor or barrister is forbidden, so as to keep things informal);

- if there are witnesses there should be an opportunity for them to be cross-examined;
- there should be an appeal structure, and a student equivalent of the 'grievance' procedure for staff, in the form of a 'complaints' procedure.

Failure to publish rules where they exist

It is commonplace for there to be *no* rules for certain situations. Often rules have not been published and, more importantly, have not been drawn to the attention of students. Or they are changed without warning. In Cambridge in 1999 the Department of Continuing Education did not know of the existence of the university's code on misconduct in research or that it was preparing a student charter and the department struggled on its own to produce a student complaints code, in ignorance of any work going on in the university at large. The *Times Higher Education Supplement* of 5 February 1999 reported that despite the award of a charter mark to Sunderland University in 1997, 'students have had problems locating copies of the university's published complaints procedures'. The second report of the Nolan Committee and the Dearing Committee's report both pressed for urgent tidying up in this area, but there were years of delay and, at the time of writing, the QAA has only just published its approved code of practice to guide universities. Universities still have no real motivation to be quick and efficient about drawing up their own versions of these rules, for once they put the rules in writing they may be called to account through the courts for failing to keep them.[24]

There is a pervasive problem that those in universities to whom the following of procedures is entrusted are often unaware of the underlying principles of fairness and, without necessarily intending injustice, short cut or muddle the sequence and deny a student under discipline a fair hearing.

'Keeping the rules' works both ways. As one judge put it, 'The applicant is entitled to the proper application of the procedures put in place for her protection.'[25] It can be very difficult to make a university keep its own rules,

---

24 See CVCP (2000) *Independent Review of Student Appeals and Staff Disputes: Interim report of the CVCP Nolan group*, CVCP, London. See Birtwhistle, T (1998) Student academic appeals: a holistic assessment, *Education and the Law*, **10**, 41–54.

25 *R v Board of Governors of Sheffield Hallam University and others, ex parte R* [1995] ELR 267 at 288.

although it can easily enforce the student's obedience to its rules by disciplining or excluding him or her.

Why is a university allowed to discipline a student?

The legal basis of the disciplinary powers of the university over students rests on the voluntary submission of the student to the rules of the institution as a condition of admission. They may be part of the student's contract with the university. That is not, as has been said, a matter in which the student as a contracting party really has any choice. The same applies if this duty of obedience is seen as a condition of membership, as it has been for generations in the older universities.[26]

The consequences to the student of breaking the rules will be at the discretion of the institution. It is likely to take some breaches more seriously than others. As long as the student does nothing to deserve expulsion the university has to go on teaching him, but it will be for the university to decide whether the misconduct is sufficiently serious to bring the student's career to an end.[27] His rights to fair decision making will not be easy to enforce, as we shall see when we get to 'remedies'.

What is a university allowed to discipline a student for?

A student can be disciplined for 'misconduct'. King's College, London, defines that in the following way:

> The essence of misconduct under this Code is improper interference, in the broadest sense, with the proper functioning or activities of the College, or with those who work or study in the College; or action which otherwise damages the College.

A list follows of actions deemed to constitute misconduct, grouped roughly under disruption and obstruction; violence and threatening or offensive behaviour; fraud and deception; action likely to cause injury; harassment;

26 If they will have one they must submit to the other. *Philips v Bury* [1692] 2 TR 346 at 358.
27 *Fitzgerald v Northcote* (1865) 4 F and F 656.

breach of the code of practice for meetings held on college premises; damage to college property; criminal offences committed on college premises or affecting other members, or damaging the good name of the college; actions bringing the college or any member or part of it into disrepute; failure to comply with a penalty already imposed under the code. Of these, the 'reputation' of the university or college is a notorious grey area for it is relatively easy to allege that reputation has been harmed.

There are different kinds of breach of the rules. Some disciplinary offences are 'academic'. A student who did not turn up for lectures or classes might in the end be expelled. The university would be relieved of its 'duty of care' if he or she did that, because the student would be preventing it from providing him or her with the teaching needed. On the other hand, if the reason for absence was that there was a serious personal difficulty with the lecturer, the student could perhaps claim that his or her absence was the university's fault, not his or her own.[28]

Plagiarism

Cheating or plagiarism is a form of academic rule breaking involving dishonesty.[29] Plagiarism is a wide-ranging offence and, to avoid doubt, all universities should give a definition to students of what they regard as plagiarism. That puts both parties on an equal footing and provides an understanding of the ground rules in cases where plagiarism is raised as an issue.

The key elements are that it must involve 'theft' of ideas or words and that it must be deliberate. That may mean cheating by borrowing or stealing an answer from someone else in an examination or assessed essay. But the whole question has become more complex with the arrival of the Internet. The *Times Higher Education Supplement* of 16 July 1999 carried the story of the discovery that students at Edinburgh appeared to have been taking material from the Internet. That may not have seemed to the students who did it to be academic dishonesty. They would probably have been encouraged to do the same thing in their school years. They may not

28 See pp 99–102.

29 'There are actions, such as cheating in examinations...which destroy...the relationship between teachers and students on which good teaching depends. They are not crimes but they cannot be tolerated because they destroy the raison d'être of a university.' Annan Report, University of Essex, 1974.

have seen it as materially different from doing their research in a library. This type of offence is certain to grow with wider access to the Internet, and it too is going to require the laying down of rules.

There can be a real failure to understand the effect of a change in the ground rules at different stages of a student's career. The move from undergraduate work in, say, history, where a student may discuss the opinions of historians second hand without adding footnotes, to graduate work, where he or she will be expected to give the source, can easily take place without anyone explaining to the student that the rules have changed, and that what was acceptable before is now plagiarism.

In the sciences, too, the situation is growing increasingly complex. A research student will normally work on a project in a team. He or she will hear conversations in which the student's seniors take part and he or she may well get to know of new ideas. Someone's chance remark may give the student an idea. If he or she then develops it, without perhaps being clear how far it is his or her own idea or prompted by someone else, then the debt ought to be acknowledged. But it would be difficult to keep a systematic record of casual conversations, or the way in which the germ of an idea may grow.

From the student's point of view probably the most important thing is that any accusation of plagiarism is made before the examiners find the student 'guilty'. 'The evidence of alleged plagiarism must be shown to the student and the student must be asked to account for the work that he or she submitted' (University of Durham, University Guidance in Respect of Plagiarism). But that often does not happen:

> A student who was one of 117 undergraduates accused of cheating by using electronic mail to copy each other's work plans to sue Edinburgh University for defamation... Miss Roe, like her fellow students, was unaware that anything was wrong until she heard about the cheating case in the media last month. She did not think it concerned her until she received a letter two days later informing her that her marks were being withheld pending an inquiry (*The Times*, 24 August 1999).

In another case, at a different Scottish university, a student was told only after the examiners had found her guilty of plagiarism and she was refused information on what she was supposed to have done so that she could try to prove her innocence.

In *R v Manchester Metropolitan University, ex parte Nolan* [1994] ELR 380 a graduate in Economics and Politics took the one year course for the Common Professional Examination (CPE), which is a conversion course taken by graduates in other subjects who wish to go on to train to be barristers or solicitors. In June 1992 he sat the examination. He took notes in with him, which the invigilators saw. An oral hearing of the Faculty Examinations Disciplinary Commitee was held, at which he denied that he had actually *referred* to the notes. Evidence was brought in the form of a psychiatric report, which the committee considered to indicate that there were mitigating circumstances. It found him guilty of attempting to gain an unfair academic advantage by bringing unauthorized material into the examination.

The decision about the penalty to be imposed was left to the CPE Board of Examiners. The Board met in September and determined the penalty without having all the papers before it and without giving the candidate an opportunity to be present or represented.

The court found that the Board had overlooked something relevant in that it had not had the evidence in mitigation before it when it made its decision about the penalty. So this case turned on a fundamental principle of fairness, which was that everything relevant must be taken into consideration when a decision is made. The case did not, in the end, test the distinction between taking material illicitly into an examination and actually using it. There were, as is so often the case, no detailed rules about what constituted plagiarism.

Kamram Beg, a student with a hitherto excellent record, went to Cambridge to study for an MPhil. One of the assessed essays was found, after the examination had been completed and the degree awarded, to contain minor plagiarism, in the form of a failure to give detailed attribution to some work, although that work had been identified in the text. He denied that the (computer-produced) essay in question was his. The university had no code on plagiarism at the time. It did not learn from this case and create one. He was disciplined; he appealed; he was stripped of his degree. He obtained leave for judicial review, but was ultimately unsuccessful because by that stage the only thing that could, technically, be pleaded, was the unfairness of having no student member on the final appeal body, which consisted solely of senior members of the academic staff and the judge did not think that enough. This again illustrates the difficulty that a student may have in challenging a decision against him where plagiarism is alleged.

The lack of procedures and a code for dealing with plagiarism can lead to extraordinary situations. One student was told that her degree classification had been lowered because of plagiarism. She asked what plagiarism had taken place. She was not told. She asked what was the evidence for it. The chairman of the examiners said that he had it on the word of his colleague. The student was given no opportunity to know of accusations against her or to defend herself.

R v South Bank University, ex parte Ifediora, 11 July 1995, concerned a student at South Bank who was given a third-class degree (although she had been expected to get a 2.2) because she was accused of plagiarism. South Bank University at the time of this case had unusually comprehensive regulations covering examination offences, including plagiarism. In this case, although the university had detailed regulations on appeals, it failed to define properly what it meant by plagiarism. There was a distinction in the regulations between alleged offences, where the Head of Department, on investigation, found that there was no case to answer; offences that were merely technical and it could reasonably be decided that no further action should be taken, and offences where there was considered to be a serious breach of the regulations.

South Bank handled such allegations by submitting them to an examination offences panel. The panel was made up of a chairman (a member of the academic staff), a member of the academic staff of a cognate department to that of the candidate, who was nominated by the dean of the faculty; a member of the academic staff of the faculty of laws; a student member.

Penalties for plagiarism were graded by South Bank University from mere reprimand to failure in the portion of the examination in which there had been plagiarism, either with or without the opportunity to retake it. In a more serious case a resit could be allowed but the mark obtained might not go above a bare pass. There was also an option of 'withholding of marks for all units taken in that diet of examinations for a specified period of time not exceeding one year'. The severest sanction was expulsion from the university. So the outcome for the student might be loss of the qualification altogether, a lower grading, or delay in knowing whether he or she had the qualification.

Appeal was allowed on procedural grounds or on the grounds that the penalty was disproportionate to the offence. The appeal was refused and the student then applied for judicial review. The court gave her leave and the university then agreed to settle the case out of court by allowing the student to resubmit the dissertation. The student resubmitted and was awarded a 2.2. That allowed her to go to law school and qualify as a solicitor.

In this university, there was a general policy of making the punishment fit the crime, so that the more serious was the plagiarism the more serious would be the penalty and there was something of a grey area between academic penalty and a general idea of fitting punishment.

But it became clear on disclosure of the papers in the ensuing litigation in the *Ifediora* case that a *policy* decision had been taken to 'make an example' of this student, so that future students would be discouraged from plagiarism. There the university overstepped the boundaries of good practice and acted unfairly in punishing one person more severely so as to discourage others.

The most recent case to reach the courts at the time of writing is *Clark v University of Lincolnshire and Humberside* [2000] CA (*The Times*, 3 May 2000). A student had been accused of plagiarism and was failed. She appealed. The academic appeals board accepted that she had not set out to deceive (the intention to deceive being a defining requirement for plagiarism) and the paper had been referred back to be remarked. The board of examiners gave it 0. The governors' appeal committee said that was not an appropriate mark and the assessment was referred back to the academic board, as the student regulations made provision should happen. The academic board then rejected the appeal. The student then had the possibility of one further attempt to take the examinations, which she did. But the regulations said that a candidate could not obtain more than a third-class degree on a resit. In 1998, she sued the university for breach of contract.

It will be clear that this is an area generating an unusual number of cases that get as far as the courts.

Disruption

Offences against the orderly running of the university form a distinct category. In the late 1960s and 1970s there was a good deal of student disruption and anxiety about that still shapes the content of disciplinary codes for students. The result is that the pre-1992 universities have disciplinary codes largely geared to dealing with problems arising out of mass action and collective disruption.[30] Some disciplinary offences of the 'disruptive' kind are against the person or against property (assault, theft) and some are serious enough to be criminal.

A different sort of 'disruptive' activity was alleged to have been committed by a student at a college of further education. The student wrote an allegedly malicious letter to a fellow student. There was a disciplinary hearing in May 1995 and she was suspended. This case raised the question of the identity of the offended party: was it the recipient of the letter or the institution? Only one side of the story was heard and the recipient of the alleged malicious letter had not made a complaint.

Criminal offences

Situations where the student is alleged to have committed an offence against the university that is also a criminal offence are a special category. Examples include a case where a student was found to have been illegally involved with guns, and another where a student distributed leaflets in the neighbourhood of the university that arguably contained incitements to racial hatred.

If there is a criminal charge, the university may hold over its internal hearing until the outcome is known. There then arises a problem of double jeopardy in that the consequence of being found guilty of a criminal charge in court may be that the university acts against the student and expels him or her, so that he or she is in effect tried and punished twice for the same offence.

'Misuse of e-mail' offences

The question of the use to which the university's students may properly put its e-mail system is a rapidly developing area of law and practice. It is touched on further here in connection with 'freedom of speech' questions and also in the student checklist (see p 114 and p 162). The basic principle involved appears to be the need for the university to be able to protect itself

30 Report of the sit-in, February 1972, and its consequences, *Cambridge University Reporter*, No 12 (14 February 1972).

as the 'publisher' (running a system allowing the e-mail to be accessed or downloaded) or 'editor' ('person' assuming editorial duties). Section 1 of the Defamation Act 1996 introduced the 'Internet defence', under which a university could seek to escape liability for libel by showing that it is not the author, editor or publisher, that it took reasonable care in relation to the publication or did not know and had no reason to believe that anything it did caused or contributed to the defamatory statement. None of that would protect the student author of the words in question from being sued for defamation where an e-mail could be accessed or downloaded.

Universities are likely to try to establish that they were involved only as operators of or providers of access to a communications system by means of which the offending words were transmitted. On the other hand, to try to prevent trouble, they might read private e-mails of students, stating that the system may be subject to monitoring at any time without notice and also make a rule that abuse of e-mail may lead to disciplinary action.

Unpaid debt

The university does not have to provide students with somewhere to live. So if they do not pay their rent that would not be a breach of their 'membership' or 'matriculation' contract. (The position may be different in Oxford and Cambridge colleges.) The problem of enforceability would be greater still if the debt was for accommodation provided by someone other than the university (for example, when the provision of accommodation was subcontracted to a company) or for a course provided by a local college only loosely linked to the university, as might be the case with a 'partner college' arrangement. The university would probably have to pursue the student for the debt through the courts in the same way as any other debt owed to it.

The non-payment of fees is a different matter, because that is a direct payment for the course that is provided. There have been a few test cases in which a university has tried to withhold the examination results when fees have not been paid. The legal principle at issue here is covered by the Unfair Terms in Consumer Contracts Regulations, 1994, which were enacted as a consequence of the Unfair Contract Terms Directive 93/13 EEC, and which have been updated since (1999). This means that a contract term will be considered 'unfair' if it causes a significant imbalance in the rights and obligations of the parties to the detriment of the consumer. This is a particularly valuable protection to students, who are not in a position to bargain about the terms and conditions when they accept a university place.

There may be another legal protection. Universities are public bodies discharging a public function (the provision of higher education) so they may not be able to refuse to make that provision because of a private debt. This is all very new, because the requirement to pay tuition fees is so recent, but there are indications that fees are going to rise, and that some universities may begin to charge additional or 'top-up' fees, and then students will begin to test some of these issues in the courts. They might even engage the provisions of the Human Rights Act about the right to education.

Student action checklist

- ✔ Is it clear what steps a student can take if he or she faces a disciplinary charge?
- ✔ Many universities now allow students university e-mail addresses (ac.uk addresses). It is important to use electronic mail in accordance with the university's code of practice, if it has one, and in any case to uphold the university's reputation and its interests by avoiding abusive language or defamatory remarks. It can be tempting to fire off an e-mail in the heat of the moment. Be careful. You could be committing a disciplinary offence.
- ✔ Are students told at the beginning of the course what will count as plagiarism? Is there a plagiarism code? Is the student given an opportunity to explain what happened if there is an accusation of plagiarism?
- ✔ What provisions does the university make about the use of material such as ready-made essays taken from the Internet?
- ✔ Does the university treat plagiarism as a disciplinary offence (behavioural, and usually punishable by fine or sending down for a period or expulsion) or an 'academic' offence (punishable by downgrading marks)?

7

The staff–student boundary

Although many student complaints are likely, directly or indirectly, to involve a member of the university's staff, this remains our shortest chapter. This is partly because of the problem of the jurisdictional divide. A student and the member of staff of a university have different contractual 'relationships' to the 'authorities' in a university. The student is (roughly) a 'customer'; the member of staff is an 'employee'. In some universities the student is a 'junior member' and the member of staff is a 'senior member'.

They are also unequal in their positions of power and influence. A member of staff could make an attractive student an offer exploiting that inequality: 'If you sleep with me, I will give you a good grade for your assessed essay.' Other members of staff will look into the matter, so it can be extremely difficult for a student to make a complaint against a member of staff with any realistic chance of success. That is another reason for the brevity of this section; comparatively few direct attempts are on record. In one case, a student complained that she and the only other student doing a course in a particular subject had been treated differently. She alleged that the other student had been 'tipped off' by the examiner about the passages for translation that were to appear on the paper. She had not. She was able to produce an e-mail from the other student admitting to this. When she tried to complain that this had put her at a disadvantage in the examination the Head of Department reacted, naturally enough, by taking soundings among his colleagues. The staff of the faculty closed ranks because the accusation, if found to be true, would have led to a serious disciplinary case against one of their number. But in any case, the Head of Department's action prejudiced any chance of a fair and independent inquiry. It can be helpful to ensure that there is a student member on any investigatory panel, but it will be uphill work to make that more than tokenism.

Harassment codes may aim to cross the staff-student barrier. 'Harassment' codes commonly try to set a benchmark of what a reasonable person would think, and speak in terms of actions or speech unwelcome to the recipient. But that, too, has its difficulties. What is welcome at one moment may cease to be so later.[1] (T-shirts have been seen, saying 'Which part of "no" is it you do not understand?')

Most students are legally adults. In personal areas, they are in charge of their own lives. There is almost certainly a duty of care deriving from the trust the student ought to be able to place in the institution. Sexual and other personal relationships will naturally be formed between teacher and taught. Members of staff may deny abusing a position of trust while admitting that there was an 'inappropriate' relationship. That creates difficulties over the degree of responsibility the institution has to ensure that students are protected from such 'abusive' relationships, especially if they risk exploiting the students' academic dependency.

A case reported in *The Independent* on 1 June 2000 involved a student who 'lodged a complaint against the tutor on her leisure and tourism course, claiming that he sexually harassed young women students in the classroom and on a field trip to Wales'. Some of the accusation turned on 'leering and ogling', some on the more precise allegation that he had 'asked female students to massage him on two occasions on a field trip in Wales'. She wrote to the Department for Education and Employment: 'I feel he is abusing his position as a teacher and there are other female students that feel this way but are too afraid to say anything.' This was a case in which it was difficult for the student complainant to have confidence in the independence of any internal college investigation, especially while fellow students who could have spoken as witnesses to the incidents continued on the course with the same teacher, which would have made it difficult for them to speak up if they wished to do so. The students' work would be 'credited' by the person they were complaining about. The complaint was eventually taken to the Further Education Funding Council, which recommended that the college considered introducing a policy and procedure

1 The 1993 AUT *Code of Conduct on Personal Relations between Staff and Students in Universities* is now out of date.

for staff on field trip visits and took action to amend its procedures to ensure that more detailed feedback was given to complainants. These improvements would not help the worried students in question, however. The episode underlines the difficulty that students can have in getting an inquiry into the behaviour of a member of staff conducted in whose handling and outcome they can have confidence, when it has to be conducted by the member of staff's colleagues, and when appeal may be available only on limited procedural grounds, with no hearing and perhaps no fresh opportunity to seek to establish the facts.

Bullying and harassment may take place not only between staff and student, but also between students, and if that happens it is probable that the university has a duty to protect the student. There are now cases in which compensation has had to be paid for bullying between pupils at school. Becky Walker brought a case against a local authority over the effects of the bullying she had endured at school as a student with cerebral palsy. She found the traumatic effects made it difficult for her to enter into the ordinary life of the other students when she began her law course at Nottingham University. She claimed that the school had not protected her.

This area is much underdeveloped in university case experience. There have been frequent complaints by students that if they have actually tried to make a complaint against a member of staff the senior staff of the institution have 'closed ranks' and made it difficult for them to get a fair hearing. The institution will often identify itself with the accused member of staff and provide legal help as though an accusation against a member of staff was against the university itself. There is also the disincentive that students rightly consider themselves to be in a vulnerable position, and rightly or wrongly fear reprisal in connection with the continuance or outcome of the course. Whether or not such fear is justified it is bound to keep a good many potential complaints unrehearsed.

Procedurally, the simplest way for universities to handle this situation is to make a separation between the jurisdiction under which a complaint from a student is considered and the disciplinary process against a member of staff that may follow if a complaint against the member of staff is upheld. There can be problems here if the student is not allowed to know what happens. There can be a perceived loss of accountability, and indeed a real loss of accountability, if nothing is seen to 'happen' when a member of staff is found to have given a student legitimate cause for complaint. One possibility is for the student to be told the outcome or sent a letter of apology, but the change of climate and practice that will be needed to encourage students to come forward in the confidence that they will be impartially heard and properly protected is likely to prove far more difficult.

Student action checklist

- ✔ What provisions does the university make to investigate any complaint that crosses the 'staff-student boundary'.
- ✔ What protection is there for the student? Is there a student member on any decision-making body that acts in such cases?

8

Complaints

'There is now a general and reasonable expectation that organisations providing services to the public should have effective systems for handling complaints.'[1]

The Quality Assurance Agency's (QAA's) guidelines were published in 2000. They reflect several uncertainties of the time. The first was the uncertainty as to whether universities would be included in the category of 'public authority' to which the Human Rights Act 1998 (HRA) applies. If so, students would be able to bring cases in which they cited the Act (although breach of the Act is not in itself a cause of action; a student could not sue on that alone). On the other hand, the vigorous recent development of the presumption that there is a contract with the student places the emphasis on the private law character of that relationship, which might rule out the use of the HRA.

The second problem was the impossibility, at the time of publication, of seeing the way forward on the idea that there would be an 'independent element' in complaints procedures. An independent stage of appeal or arbitration or mediation would take matters outside the university. The university need not consent to that because it is autonomous. This is an extremely important limitation for students, who frequently find that their complaints are not addressed effectively or in a timely way inside the institution and actively seek some regulatory authority that can intervene. They report bewilderment at finding that the QAA, the Higher Education

1 Quality Assurance Agency (2000) *QAA Code of Practice: Academic appeals and student complaints on academic matters*, Quality Assurance Agency, Gloucester.

Funding Councils, the Department for Education and Employment, and their MPs, are equally powerless to intervene, however bad the situation is.

There was a third limitation to the scope of the QAA Code. The QAA itself had a limited remit. Accordingly, the QAA code defines a complaint as 'any specific concern about the provision of a programme of study or related academic service'. But the introduction stresses the need 'to ensure that there are no unjustifiable inconsistencies or incompatibilities between the way they deal with academic and non-academic complaints and appeals'. It is recognized that the range of possible complaints that students may reasonably wish to raise is much wider.

What is a complaint?

A complaint is not the same as an appeal. A complaint is about the way in which the university or its staff or students have behaved towards the student or about a breach of the 'undertakings' in the contract it made with the student. An appeal is against a decision already taken, which adversely affects the student, such as a decision to discipline him or her or remove him or her from a course, or against the outcome of an examination.

The history of modern student complaints procedures

To obtain a picture of the history behind the way the QAA tackled its task, we need to go back into the late 1990s. The Dearing Committee made recommendations about the handling of complaints from students. The government's *Response to Dearing, Higher Education for the 21st Century*, included Dearing's Recommendation 60 and its own response, in a hearty endorsement of the view that something urgently needed to be done:

> Recommendation 60:
> We recommend to institutions that, over the next two years, they review and, if necessary, amend their arrangements for handling complaints from students, to ensure that they reflect the principles of natural justice; they are transparent and timely; they include procedures for reconciliation and arbitration; they include an independent, external element; and they are managed by a senior member of staff.

> The Government regards it as important that, as the Committee recommends, institutions should review their procedures for handling student complaints, and amend them if they do not meet certain criteria, including an independent external element. The Government encourages institutions to take the necessary action in the light of the guidance to be issued shortly by the Committee of Vice-Chancellors and Principals and intends to review, in two years' time, whether sufficient progress has been made.

The two years had all but elapsed when the Department for Education and Employment wrote to the Committee of Vice-Chancellors and Principals (CVCP) on 10 February 1999. A link was made in the letter with Dearing's Recommendation 25 'that the new Quality Assurance Agency should develop a fair and robust system for complaints relating to educational provision'. In the same letter, the government's reply on that point was quoted: 'The QAA intends to follow up serious problems over educational provision or standards, though the primary responsibility for acting on individual complaints should continue to rest with the institution concerned.'

Despite all the strong talk and promises, there has been a good deal of 'sitting on hands'. The CVCP was waiting for the QAA. Individual institutions were waiting for both. The DfEE was waiting for individual institutions to put their house in order. As late as 1 June 2000, Lucy Hodges was writing in *The Independent*: 'The Vice-Chancellors are doing the minimum and hoping it will avoid an expensive lawsuit.' In one case she cites (in a further education college) the complainant 'received a letter saying simply that staff and students had been interviewed and the matter would not be taken further'. That is a typical response. Institutions conduct any inquiry largely behind the scenes and seek if possible to let the matter lie.

The survey carried out by the National Postgraduate Committee and the Union of UEA Students

So we need to go back further still, to underline the difficulty in changing the climate of expectation. In 1998 Don Staniford, a former PhD student at the University of East Anglia, conducted a survey of the complaints procedures in UK universities.[2] He found that surprisingly few had any complaints

2 Informally circulated and submitted to regulatory bodies.

procedures at all; 34 per cent had no procedures; 75 per cent reported that complaints were increasing; 91 per cent had received solicitors' letters about student complaints. Only 30 per cent claimed that their procedures were coping and 19 per cent that they were 'effective'. Only 8 per cent had provision for resort to an 'independent person'.[3]

The survey found that most complaints are about supervision or teaching, followed by complaints about academic assessment and examination failure. A smaller number of complaints concerned 'quality of life' in the university: facilities and resources, accommodation, unpleasant treatment by staff or other students, poor communications, financial issues, with a tiny 3 per cent in the Staniford survey complaining of discrimination or harassment, although that is an area where most institutions have well-developed codes. Staniford found that 70 per cent of his respondents reported that their complaints procedures were 'not coping'. He found, strikingly, that most institutions have an appeal procedure and that it is usually well developed. At one university it is 20 pages long, with an 'Academic Complaints Procedure' of a single page to go with it.

The NUS Good Practice Guides

The National Union of Students (NUS) *Good Practice Guides* set out a series of student 'rights' for universities to respect when students make complaints. The first is a right to make a complaint, without fear of being subjected to discipline for doing so. The second is a right to act as a group, where several complainants have the same complaint.

The third is a right to information about the grounds on which complaints may be made and the procedures by which they should be handled. That goes with a right to be told what the timetable for handling a complaint will be, for there is also a right to a response in a reasonable time.

Next comes the right to an independent judgement. If there is no such right the institution is acting as judge in its own case. That is particularly important where the institution claims powers to stop a complaint from progressing or to deem it frivolous or vexatious.

There is a right to representation. The student should be told that he or she can be accompanied at any hearing, either by someone who will support

3 Acknowledgement to Don Staniford for these figures.

him or her and act as a witness to the conduct of the proceedings, or by someone who will speak for him or her.

There is a right to a fair hearing. The case-law of the United Kingdom is likely to support an institution in allowing the academic staff who have been involved in the events that have led to the complaint taking part in the review of the complaint. European cases tend to go the other way, however, and it is likely that this will become less acceptable in the United Kingdom.

There is a right to an appropriate remedy. That might mean restoring the student to the position he or she was in before the problem began; awarding the degree; doing what the 'contract' requires; or damages.

Legal requirements

In any case, there are legal requirements. There is a contract, so any express terms of the contract between student and university have to be honoured. There is also an implied contractual duty to treat the student fairly and not to breach the Unfair Terms in Consumer Contracts Regulations 1994.

There is a 'public law' dimension, because most universities are in part publicly funded public bodies, so they have to meet public law standards of fairness, and the university has to act reasonably, although, as we have just seen, that can easily be thwarted by the autonomy of universities. Under the Sex Discrimination, Race Relations and Disability Acts, complaints procedures must not discriminate and the student must not suffer victimization as a result of making a complaint of discrimination. The Data Protection Act 1998 will enlarge rights of access to documentary material, but not to their fullest extent (including manual records) until the autumn of 2001. The Public Interest Disclosure Act does not cover students because it is an employment provision, but the CVCP is encouraging universities to create codes applying to students as well as to staff.

The Freedom of Information Act may be helpful, though the signs are not encouraging:

> By sleight of hand, freedom of information to all as of right is transformed into the civil servant's or university administrator's freedom to retain information. In the QAA draft code, 'full access' to 'all relevant documentation' has become 'appropriate access' to 'relevant documentation'. Under the proposed revision, universities will retain discretion to judge

> the appropriateness of disclosure and the relevance of the documentation it may choose to disclose to the student. How is the student to judge whether the university has acted reasonably in making these judgements, untainted by its interest in defending its position in relation to a complaint?[4]

Under the Human Rights Act 1998 there is likely to be a statutory requirement to act in accordance with the European Convention on Human Rights, which may at least make universities take the basics of fair procedure seriously and provide for:

- publication of step by step transparent procedures;
- creating the expectation that problems will be resolved quickly and informally where possible;
- providing informed independent help for the student complainant or appellant both at the beginning and when a complaint or appeal reaches the formal stage;
- helping the student to identify the problem(s) the procedures can address;
- providing a list of grounds for complaint or appeal;
- ensuring speedy handling of complaints or appeals;
- disclosure of documents, including examination papers;
- ensuring independent adjudication;
- providing written reasons for the decision;
- providing an independent 'ombudsman' if the student remains aggrieved when the formal procedures have been exhausted;
- providing speedy and effective remedies.

When to complain

The student should complain early on when a problem arises. There are reasons for urgency. The first is that the institution may try to argue that the student cannot really have anything to complain about or the complaint would have been made at an earlier stage. Failing to complain at the outset will be held against the student in later internal procedures or by the courts.

4 Letter from Neil McDougall, *Times Higher Education Supplement*, 6 August 1999.

For example, a student who says, after failing an examination, that he was badly supervised will be told that he should have brought that to the university's attention before he took the exam.

Secondly, if the complaint is not nipped in the bud, the problem is likely to get worse and more pride and face-saving will be involved for the institution, so the problem will become 'bigger' and therefore harder to resolve.

There is also the question of having 'standing' to complain. Once a student has left the university it will not necessarily have to entertain his complaints and it may say that it intends to ignore them. That can cover appeals too. An academic registrar advised a student that 'once a student has graduated, no appeal is allowed', although he admitted that there might be 'grounds for a restrospective claim where the student was not made aware of the regulations'.[5]

On the other hand, complaining can make a bad situation worse. Some students have complained that the attitudes of lecturers towards them have deteriorated when it is known that they have made a complaint. In one case, lecturers in the faculty refused to teach a student at all after a complaint had been made (and the complaint was never investigated).

The university should be ready to undertake that no discretion finally or summarily to dismiss a complaint shall rest with any officer within the university, without a properly conducted inquiry or hearing. Students should not be advised against using a procedure where it exists 'because it will get people's backs up', although this often occurs. Complaining, raising concern or appealing must be 'protected' acts, so that the student does not fear to speak up and has somewhere to go for help if there is reprisal.

It may not be easy for a student who has made a complaint to keep to the rule that it is important to carry on with work as usual on the course while a complaint is investigated and to try to keep the complaint and the study separate. There is inevitably stress and anxiety and fear, which may badly affect a student's work.

The university should recognize a duty to investigate complaints promptly, so as to keep this kind of damage and difficulty to a minimum. It is rare for a university to be efficient in this respect. It is best to deal with the complaint as close as possible to where the problem starts. It is important to 'manage' a complaint quickly and effectively. Unless a complaint is

5 Staniford Survey (unpublished).

disposed of quickly in that way, it is liable to rumble on and on, sometimes for years, with the university becoming more and more defensive, as it comes to believe it is defending its own officers and its own reputation and loses sight of the question whether it has been fair to the student. It is not, as has already been noted, uncommon for it to take several years to look into a student's representations.

Students should be aware of these realities before they begin on the process of making a formal complaint. But if too many are put off even trying, the system will not improve.

The university that is receiving a growing number of complaints should take that as an indicator of falling standards of teaching or administration or both. That also makes it important for it to take remedial steps with the greatest possible speed.

What to complain about

A student may reasonably complain about anything that the university has an obligation to do or provide – or to prevent – in connection with the provision of the course, or the examinations that have to be taken to get the qualification for which the student is registered. That includes anything the institution provides, or fails to provide, by way of buildings or equipment. It can extend, as we have seen earlier, into areas where the student's health or safety is put at risk, or where other people the university is 'responsible for' are making it difficult for the student to study.

The following is a working list. It will be relatively easy to deal with some of these types of complaint by making better provision across the board. But they will not always come separately; many students do not speak up until their situations have become complicated by more than one of these factors.

Worries about being properly prepared for the examination

- I do not know what is expected of me on this course.
- I do not think this is a very good course (standards).
- My supervisor is missing supervisions/not marking my essays or giving me oral comments on them.
- Lectures are being cancelled.

- Lectures are inaudible; are confusing.
- I came here especially for this element in the course and the lecturer running it has left.

Worries about academic and educational support and resources

- No one gives me any sense of how well I am getting on; there is no warning system if I am likely to fail.
- I do not know who to turn to when I am worried about my work.
- No one told me where to find the learning resources for this project/piece of work.
- There are not enough computers in college/the faculty to meet student demand/the library shuts too early.

Examination and assessment

- I was disadvantaged in taking the examination and I did not get the proper allowance of extra time/special facilities.
- I did mention my medical problem but my supervisor/tutor did not pass the message on.
- There was no independent examiner.
- The examiners took irrelevant considerations into account.

Plagiarism, intellectual property

- My supervisor stole my ideas/test results.
- I want to publish my findings but this research project is commercially funded and my thesis is subject to a confidentiality agreement.

Human relations (many universities have a counselling service which probably ought to be the first port of call for this kind of concern)

- I do not like my director of studies/supervisor/tutor.
- My director of studies/supervisor/tutor does not like me.
- My director of studies/supervisor/tutor has been making sexual advances to me.
- My director of studies/supervisor/tutor told me I would get a good mark if I went to bed with him/her.
- My director of studies/supervisor/tutor makes remarks that make me feel diminished.
- My director of studies/supervisor/tutor is a bully.

- One of my fellow students has been bullying me.
- I have been raped.
- I have been accused of rape but I thought she had consented.

Discrimination

- I have suffered disadvantages because I am a girl/boy/from an ethnic minority/disabled.
- There are some societies I can't join because I am a girl/boy/from an ethnic minority/disabled.
- My head of department has never given a postgraduate studentship to a girl/boy/someone from an ethnic minority/someone disabled.

Health and safety

- I can't concentrate when I want to study in my room because of the noise from the college bar.
- I think my friend is HIV positive; a hepatitis carrier. Should I tell someone?
- I broke my leg on the college football pitch.
- I don't think it is a good idea for my tutor to give drinks parties at which everyone gets drunk.
- There are people working in our lab who have nothing to do with the university. They work for the head of department's spinout company.
- There are not enough fume cupboards/Bunsen burners for the students.
- What was that rumour about asbestos in the arts and social science building?

Problems involving staff who are not members of the university

- The cleaners keep upsetting my experiments by dusting round them.
- The porters took away our aerosols by force when we sprayed rude words on the walls in the porters' lodge. They assaulted us.

Breaches of published procedures or the rules of natural justice or unreasonable delay

- I don't know where to find the procedures. Are they published anywhere?
- Has the person considering my complaint had any training in how to do it fairly?

- I don't think I got a fair hearing. What can I do?
- Why has it taken two years for my complaint to be dealt with?

The complaints code embodying all this should be published and students should each be given a copy. It should be understandable and clear, should make provision for proper investigation and should offer real remedies.

There should not be conflict or overlap with other procedures in the institution. There should be guidance on which procedure to 'use' for a given complaint. Many universities have introduced harassment codes without working out how they are to fit in with existing discipline and grievance codes. 'There is the problem of "bouncing" where no one will take responsibility for dealing with a complaint, with the obvious solution that all institutions ought to have at least a back-stop complaints officer.'[6]

The need for training

It is extremely important for the university to train those who are to handle complaints. Complaints procedures are repeatedly mishandled by individuals who do not understand the rules or believe it to be their duty to find in favour of the university, and that can make things worse. Whatever their role, all members of staff should be required to undergo training in the identification and handling of student complaints and appeals before they are allowed to have any part in dealing with them.

'Triage' is a method used in hospital accident and emergency departments for taking a preliminary look at a case to decide what issues it raises. The first need is to identify the problem. A complaint often includes all sorts of elements, which may need tackling in different ways:

- The student may need help in identifying and focusing on the grounds for complaint (a judicial task).
- The student may need 'counselling' (a pastoral task).
- The student may need help in identifying the person to approach in the first instance for advice (an administrative task).

6 Farrington, D (1994) *The Law of Higher Education*, Butterworths, London.

It is essential that these roles are kept separate in everyone's minds.

A 'first instance' team can be set up, cooperatively with the students' union, competent to operate a system of 'triage', to help the student identify the problem, and to explain the routes to a solution that may be open. All students can be provided with a list of names of these specially trained members of the academic staff or administrative staff to whom they can go at the outset. Various 'officers' can have a role in such a system, such as a complaints officer, or there could be a staff-student liaison committee (although these are sometimes toothless).

The statement of complaint

1. Describe what has happened to cause you to complain, giving dates and times and any details you can. You will need to show that something has gone wrong in the discharge of a duty the university or college had towards you, and that you have suffered as a result. The complainant must be the student affected, or several affected students acting together, or someone directly affected complaining on behalf of a group of students similarly affected.
2. Give the names of the person(s) you are complaining against or explain what action of a body or committee has given rise to the complaint.
3. Give the names of any witnesses who have agreed to support you, enclosing a signed note from each of them to say that you have their consent to give their names.
4. Enclose any documentary evidence, keeping a copy for yourself. If there are more than ten pages, provide a list of contents and number the pages. Get a signed written statement if you can. Anonymous 'witness statements' are not likely to carry much weight.
5. Say what action you would like to be taken or what remedy you are seeking.
6. Give the name of the person who has agreed to accompany or support or represent you at any meeting or hearing, or make a request to be provided with such a supporter.

Student action checklist

- ✔ You should be able to rely on the university having a code or procedure for dealing with student complaints which is in tune with the ground-rules laid down by the QAA in 2000.
- ✔ Ask the university for its complaints procedures and its disciplinary procedures for students. Compare them and point out any imbalance in provision between the two. Most universities have well-established disciplinary codes but have only recently begun work on the creation of complaints procedures.
- ✔ Is it clear to a student what steps to take if he or she wants to make a complaint?
- ✔ Complain promptly, but in moderate language.
- ✔ Ask what protections are in place to ensure that you do not suffer reprisal as a result of making a complaint.
- ✔ Meetings to seek to resolve complaints are a good idea. Students should make notes of such meetings and ask for copies of any minutes taken. It may be possible to ask to tape-record the meeting.

9

Getting help

A university should provide somewhere for students to go with problems. A counselling service can be helpful, but most such services are geared to giving help with student distress and they may not be able to clarify where to begin to address a difficulty with the university's own conduct. On one side of the gap in provision that is often left stands the local students' union.

The students' union

The students' union is separate from the university.[1] Each university makes its own agreement with its students' organization, sometimes in its charter or statutes, sometimes by ordinance. Universities are autonomous and so there is no general set of 'rights' of students' unions common to all universities. Legislation in the Education Act 1944 imposed duties on universities and other institutions in relation to which students' unions have been established. The governing bodies of universities have a duty to ensure that certain requirements are met (s22(2)). The union must have a written constitution, which is to be reviewed by the institution at least every five years. There must be a provision that a student has a right not to belong to the union and a right to say that he or she does not want to be

1 The law regards it as a charity (see Hyams, O (1998) *Law of Education*, Sweet & Maxwell, p 524 ff). The students' union is an unincorporated body of persons, which is not a legal entity (like a club or friendly society). A students' union cannot have objectives that conflict with the charitable educational purposes of the university. The officers or committee may be able to sue or be sued or to enter into contracts.

represented by it. A student also has a right not to be unfairly disadvantaged because he or she has exercised that right. There must be elections by secret ballot to major union offices, with all members having a right to vote. There is also a limit on the period for which an individual student may hold paid sabbatical office. There are further requirements to ensure proper conduct of the union's financial affairs.

In practice this means that, in most universities, the institution (through its council or senate) approves the constitution of the students' union. The university will frequently supervise the financial affairs of the union. Often there is a staff-student committee or board.

There is also the National Union of Students, which is independent of any particular university and that produces such documents as the *Good Practice Guides on Complaints and Academic Appeals* (National Union of Students, Higher Education Campaign, 1998). The stated purpose of these guides is 'to help union officers lobby for improvements to the institution's procedures', during a period when they will be put together in some institutions for the first time, or reviewed in 'Nolan' and 'Dearing' terms in others and, as is pointed out, 'Once [they are] reviewed and amended...it will be very difficult to alter the procedures governing complaints and appeals'.

What can students' unions do?

Representation of student interests is the central purpose of the student union. It can lobby, try to influence policy and give out information. (Liaison with university authorities requires tact and diplomacy, but too much tact may result in inaction on the part of the university.)

Provision of support for individual students (advice, someone to accompany them to hearings) is the second main area of student union support. That may include providing legal assistance or representation, but finance for that is likely to be extremely limited.

The students' union has sabbatical officers, usually including a welfare officer, who can accompany or represent students who need help. But its officers are usually relatively young and it may not be easy for them to get on the necessary terms of familiarity with the university's officers and its governance in their own year's term of office to make them effective at unscrambling student issues.

Statutory and other bodies with relevant responsibilities

We turn now to the other side of the gap, to national and outside bodies.

The Department for Education and Employment

The Department for Education and Employment is the section of the civil service with responsibility for education matters. A letter to an MP or to the Secretary of State for Education will probably find its way there for a reply. But no direct action is likely to be possible. There are no powers to intervene in the affairs of universities at the level of individual student problems except in the courts.

The Higher Education Funding Councils

The Higher Education Funding Councils were created under the Further and Higher Education Act 1992. Their remit is financial. Section 65(1) makes them 'responsible for the administration of funds made available to them by the Secretary of State and others for the purpose of providing financial support for various activities'. The Act allows room for the addition of 'supplementary' functions (s69).

Again, the hands of Higher Education Funding Councils are tied by an inability to act in individual cases. They can 'punish' institutions by withholding funding, but they cannot intervene on behalf of students in dispute with their universities. Sir Ron Dearing made the point that 'the funding bodies should be enabled to withdraw funding if the complaint is upheld and appropriate remedial action is not forthcoming' (*The Independent*, 28 August 1998).

The Quality Assurance Agency (QAA)

The QAA was set up in succession to the Higher Education Quality Council and it is 'co-owned' by the Committee of Vice-Chancellors and Principals (CVCP), now 'Universities UK', and the Higher Education Funding Councils.

The DfEE's Charter for Higher Education gave the impression to students that the then Higher Education Quality Council would be able to investigate individual complaints. The QAA, which replaces it, has a greatly enlarged remit, but it, too, has no authority to intervene, no powers to investigate individual complaints and it cannot act as an appellate body when things go wrong between a university and a student.

'The Quality Assurance Agency does not have and does not seek a role in adjudicating on individual student complaints. It is for institutions to put in place fair, open and robust systems to handle complaints,' said John Randall, Chief Executive of the QAA in a letter to the *Times Higher Education Supplement*, 18 September 1998.

Universities UK (The Committee of Vice-Chancellors and Principals (CVCP))

Universities UK (the former CVCP) is an association of the Chief Executives of UK universities. The Committee of Vice-Chancellors and Principals *Management Guidance*, April 1998, said: 'It is extremely important that every university should have a suitable internal complaints machinery for students which is widely known and can be easily invoked'. It, too, has no brief, however, nor any authority to examine individual complaints or to intervene in actual disputes.

The media

The media can help by putting extremely public pressure on the institution, but the media can be uncertain allies. They may harm a cause as much as help it. They may also inadvertently harm a student's prospects for the future. The much-publicized case of Laura Spence, the schoolgirl from a comprehensive school rejected by Magdalen College, Oxford, was in the press for several weeks in May and June 2000. Her name may be remembered when she eventually qualifies and wants to begin her career. A student can easily become notorious.

Voluntary bodies

A number of voluntary bodies will help students with advice and support, but, again, they have no power to intervene and can only write letters and try to encourage universities to examine the complaint.

Getting legal advice

Students may be able to get legal aid, but even at the initial stages of finding out whether there is a case that can be taken to the courts there is a danger of running into considerable expense. Not all solicitors have the specialist experience to give the best advice in this area, and students who go to a local or family solicitor may spend a good deal without getting the help they need.

Student action checklist

- ✔ Know where you stand legally as early as possible. Seek advice from a specialist in education law and know your legal rights and remedies.
- ✔ Students will normally be eligible for free advice under the Legal Help and Assistance scheme.
- ✔ What does the university do about ensuring that student union sabbatical officers and other student representatives are able to serve on university committees?
- ✔ What are the categories of reserved business from which students are excluded? Why?
- ✔ Does the university open training and 'staff development' courses to student officers?

10

Remedies

Internal and external remedies

One of the most confusing areas for students in difficulties is the question of what is an 'internal' and what is an 'external' place to go for a remedy. It is important that all the avenues of appeal within the university are exhausted before the student tries to go outside it for a remedy. A student at Liverpool John Moores who was prevented from proceeding from the second to the final year of a BSc in pharmacy went through a series of appeals at which the same committee reconsidered her case and on no occasion had she been allowed to attend. But there was a further level of appeal open to her, at which she could have appeared in person, and before she attempted that she went to court. Although Collins J criticized the complexity of the university's procedures, she was refused leave for judicial review because he held that she had an obligation to exhaust the internal appeal first.[1]

It may not be easy to discover what order to take the 'internal' procedures in, or even whether they have indeed all been exhausted. The university has a duty to make that clear if the student asks. In *R v Leeds Metropolitan University, ex parte Manders* [1998] ELR 502 it was far from clear what the student ought to have done. He was awarded a pass degree and he said that one of his tutors had marked him down because he was biased. He requested a review of the decision, referring the board of examiners to his grievance application. A few days later he put in a grievance, but he did not give it to the right person and he did not name the tutor in question. He

1 *R v Liverpool John Moores University, ex parte Hayes* [1998] ELR 261.

supplied the name a week later, but by then the board of examiners had made its decision that his appeal could not be considered because he had not given proper details of the mitigating circumstances he alleged. The deputy vice-chancellor rejected his complaint that the board of examiners' review body ought to have asked him for clarification of the connection between the grievance and the appeal before rejecting his appeal, and that, since it knew there was a connection, it ought not to have taken its decision until the grievance had been resolved.

Mr Manders sought judicial review, but he left it beyond the three-month limit. The court ultimately found against him, although it recognized that it was arguable that there had been procedural impropriety, partly because he had delayed in bringing his application for leave for judicial review.

That takes us to another problem area. Although the student must always exhaust internal avenues before going to court, time-limits on applications to courts laid down by statute must not be exceeded, because then the student in search of a remedy will have the additional task of persuading the court to allow the case to be considered even though it is 'out of time'. The main statutory time limits a student needs to know are the three-month limit for judicial review, where it is important to get the application in as quickly as possible after the offending 'decision' so as to be seen to have acted 'decisively', and the six-year limit for alleged breaches of the university's contract with the student.

This also takes us to a further question. When does a complaint or appeal have to stop? When has everything been done that can be done? It is so common for universities to frustrate attempts to get a complaint or concern addressed that it is important to ensure that students are not prevented from getting reasonable satisfaction. For example, even though something may have been investigated under one process, aspects of the problem may not have come to light that might do so in a more rigorous investigation under another head. Where a public authority has instigated an appeal process, it creates a presumption that the process will be judicially conducted. An appeals process that serves no purpose and exists to promote public relations is a misrepresentation that can give rise to estoppel (*R v West Glamorgan County Council, ex parte Gheissary, The Times*, 18 December 1985).

This kind of thing is common in universities' conduct of their procedures.

> What would be the point of giving someone a right to be heard, while denying him any knowledge as to what he was to be heard about.
>
> (*Malloch v Aberdeen Corp* [1971] 1 WLR 1578)

> I feel bound to express my prima facie dislike of a situation in which the tribunal has before it a document...which has not been seen by a party which will be affected by the tribunal.
>
> (*Wiseman v Bourneman* [1971] AC 279)

These observations have to be set against the common-sense rule that finality is important. A case cannot be allowed to run on and on, from appeal to appeal, indefinitely. Students eventually have to 'get on with their life', even if the problem remains unresolved. The longer a dispute goes on the tougher it gets. The institution is much richer and more powerful than the individual student.

It is at this stage, when things may have gone badly wrong with the handling of the complaint or appeal, or when the student's sense of injustice is not appeased by an investigation even when it has been properly conducted, that the matter teeters on the edge between the internal and external avenues of recourse. For the student at an 'old' university, that is one that had its beginnings before 1992, there is a final avenue of 'internal' appeal that has to be used, and one which in effect blocks the way to the courts.

The visitor

What is a visitor?

Visitors began centuries ago as officers appointed to ensure that the wishes of a funder of a charitable body continue to be carried out after his or her death. They could deal with disputes if they were invited to do so and they could interpret the 'domestic laws' created by the founder if they turned out to be unclear. The 'chartered' universities (those older than 1992), except Oxford and Cambridge, have visitors. Oxford and Cambridge colleges have visitors, but not the universities themselves, which can make it difficult for a student to know where to go for help, because a student is a member both of the college and of the university. The 'new' universities (the ones that were polytechnics until 1992) do not have visitors, although in some cases they have an officer called the visitor. That is because they were set up under statute and are therefore 'statutory' and not 'domestic' bodies.[2]

At the University of Hertfordshire a PhD student wanted to challenge a decision. She tried to use the university's internal procedures to appeal and in the end she sought to go to its visitor. But this was a post-1992 university and although it had an officer it called a visitor, that was really a mere label. A 'real' visitor cannot be invented by a post-1992 university.

Exclusivity of jurisdiction

Exclusivity of jurisdiction is the rule that if there is a visitor there is no avenue by which a student can go to court.[3] The dispute has to go to the visitor. This means that some students, those at post-1992 universities, can go to court about the same problems that a student in an 'old' university would have to take to the visitor. So it results in inequality of treatment. *Casson v University of Aston in Birmingham* [1983] 1 All ER 88 at 91 points out that no visitor has ever awarded damages, so the visitor system does not offer a remedy that is a real alternative to a case for breach of contract.

The courts have had to wrestle with the 'exclusivity question' a good deal over the years. There are some recent examples. The outcome of *R v Judicial Committee for the University of London, ex parte Vijayatunga* [1988] 2 WLR 1106, where a research student petitioned the visitor when he was denied the PhD degree, limited visitorial powers but not in such a way as to create an avenue of recourse to the courts in such circumstances. It was held that 'the court has a supervisory but not an appellate jurisdiction' in regard to the visitor of the University of London (at 516). *Casson*, however, seemed to establish that a visitor does not have jurisdiction in a matter

2 In *R v Visitors to Middle Temple, ex parte Bullock* [1996] ELR 349 at 355 it was said that a visitor had an untrammelled jurisdiction to investigate wrongs and that it could be exercised in any way which was felt to be appropriate. The visitor could still not interfere with academic judgement, however.

3 With some exceptions, set out in s206 of the Education Reform Act 1988.

governed by the common law, so if there is a contract there may be no visitorial jurisdiction.[4]

In practice, the lengthy and solid list of precedents about the visitor's jurisdiction is likely to prevail. There is a long history of cases involving visitors, going back to *Philips v Bury* [1692] 2 TR 346. The courts have repeatedly said that they cannot interfere where there is a visitor, because he has exclusive jurisdiction over the 'domestic' affairs of the institution. The only exception is where the visitor has acted unfairly or made some procedural mistake in handling the case. In *Pearce v University of Aston* [1991] 2 All ER 461, CA, three lecturers at the University of Aston, who were among staff made compulsorily redundant, applied for an injunction to restrain the University from acting in breach of its statutes. The lecturers sought to rely on s206 of the Education Reform Act 1988. It was held that the court has jurisdiction under the Education Reform Act 1988 until a reference has been made to and accepted by the visitor, but then the visitor's jurisdiction is exclusive.

Even a visitor himself may not be clear whether he has jurisdiction, as happened in the case of the visitor of Sidney Sussex College in *Oakes v Sidney Sussex College, Cambridge* [1988] 1 All ER 1004, where the court in the end sent the matter back to the visitor to deal with.

Is a visitor a good thing?

Apart from this obvious drawback for a student who is keen to get his or her case heard by a court, on the face of it, a visitor ought to be a good thing. This is an officer to whom a student can go with a problem, without having to face a bill for legal fees. (On the other hand, a student cannot get legal aid to pay for legal help with a petition to a visitor.)

Getting to the visitor

He or she may find that it is difficult to get to the visitor, however. The university may try to put barriers in the way, either by not telling the student about the existence of the visitor, or by not explaining how to appeal to the visitor. One student spent months in 1998–99 writing to the registrar to try

4 Smith, Peter M (1981) The exclusive jurisdiction of the University visitor (1981) 97 LQR 610 at 615.

to obtain clarification of the status and role of the 'visitor' and of her rights to submit her petition.

For even when the student is told about the visitor there may be attempts to prevent the visitor actually being approached. In theory, anyone who is a 'corporator', or member, of a chartered university can go to the visitor with a problem, and the whole university can make an 'official' approach, for example, if it needs an interpretation of one of its internal laws to settle a disagreement about its application. Sometimes a university will even try to prevent a student making an appeal at all, or try to put blockages in the way of appeal to a visitor, by telling the student that it can be done only through the university's administration or that the problem is not one that the visitor can consider, or that it is too late.

The student should never take 'no' for an answer. The student should ask who the visitor is and request a copy of the regulations that cover appeal to the visitor. He or she has a right to see them, and also a right to know if the university does not have any, as may well be the case. In any case, the student can write to the visitor, enclosing the correspondence and can explain that he or she wishes to make an appeal but no one seems to be clear how you should do it. Where the visitor is the Queen the student simply writes to the Queen at Buckingham Palace and the Palace staff will always deal with the matter by referring it to the Privy Council or the Lord Chancellor, whichever is appropriate.

The second hurdle is that, because the visitor is usually the Queen or sometimes an archbishop or bishop, this means in practice that there is an apparatus of delegation of the tasks of the visitor and the petitioner finds herself corresponding with the Privy Council office or the Lord Chancellor's office.

Neil McDougall, a post-graduate student, took a case against the University of Bath to the visitor, and found to his surprise that there were no procedures he could be handed and that there was delay while someone was found to look into the case. He received a letter from the Lord Chancellor's department confirming that the Queen was the visitor for his University and explaining what would happen:

> There is no fixed procedure, and the flexibility and informality are among the advantages of the visitatorial system. Nevertheless, it is convenient for the majority of cases...to follow the same pattern. The proceedings are launched by a petition to the Visitor...The petition does not have to be in

> any special form... What is important is that the complaint should be set out clearly, indicating all acts or omissions of which complaint is made and any rules or regulations alleged to have been broken. Copies of those, and of any relevant correspondence, should be supplied and their relevance explained. The petition should also specify exactly what it is that the petitioner is asking the Visitor to do.

Normally, both sides are at least given an opportunity to comment, the university on what the petitioner has said and the petitioner on the university's reply. Even if there are some ready-made procedures, they may be sketchy. One PhD student at the University of Essex took a complaint to the visitor and although this university, unusually, had a 'note of guidance on appeals to the visitor' to give her, she found it difficult to proceed without help. The note, signed by Lord Slynn, on behalf of the Queen as visitor, was clear and kept to the essentials, but a person without legal experience could easily be in difficulties about identifying 'grounds'. A student will not be likely to get any help in framing the complaint. There may be no hearing at which the problem can be clarified.

That may not be the worst of a student's problems, however. One student was told that her supervisor would not give her the necessary support for the continuation of her research unless she withdrew her complaint against him. She did so. Her supervisor then used the same tactic to get her to withdraw the complaint she had laid against another member of staff. She was then told that while the matter was under investigation she would not be considered for the allocation of graduate student teaching (the denial of which, she believed, was in reprisal against her for an earlier complaint about a mistake over her fee status, which had been the substance of her original complaint to the visitor). This case illustrates a common problem: the visitor system is simply not well run, by universities and often by the visitors themselves. The Universities and Colleges Education Law Network (UCELNET) group has been working on the creation of guidelines for visitors' use, and for universities themselves to use in connection with resort to visitors.

Can the visitorial system be allowed to continue?

It looks as though the visitorial system will fall foul of the 1998 Human Rights Act, because there is no requirement about fair procedure and the process is usually in practice (although not in theory) slow and secretive. The Human Rights Act, article 6, gives everyone 'in the determination of his civil rights' an entitlement to a 'fair and public hearing within a reasonable time' by an independent and impartial tribunal established by law. For the purposes of the Act, the visitor cannot be an independent tribunal because he or she is, by definition, internal to the structure of this 'domestic body' of whose laws he or she is the appointed guardian.[5] Because the visitor's jurisdiction excludes that of the courts, he or she may not count as being 'established by law'. As we see, not all visitors provide details of their procedure to appellants. Not all universities or colleges with visitors notify staff and students of their right to go to the visitor or allow them to do so directly. There is at present no consistency in the procedures used by visitors, and therefore no guarantee of a fair hearing; indeed it is unusual for there to be a hearing at all. If there is not a rapid statutory change a university may find itself in court defending its visitor at considerable public expense. It might now take no more than a single case to overturn this ancient jurisdiction.

It is manifestly unfair that some students have an avenue of recourse before they have to go to court whereas others do not; it is equally obviously unfair that some students are denied access to the courts at all.

Alternatives to the visitor

An ombudsman

In Canada each university has its own officer called an 'ombudsman'. At present there is no university or higher education ombudsman in the United Kingdom. The National Union of Students *Good Practice Guide on Complaints*, 1998, argued that the establishment of a national higher education ombudsperson would have a number of points in its favour. It would provide a remedy which would cost the complainant nothing and where there would be no fear of liability for the costs of the other party. It could be arranged for neither side to use lawyers and for the process to be inquisitorial if that was appropriate. The process would be publicly accountable,

5 *Times Higher Education Supplement*, 4 May 1999, carried an important article on this question.

with an annual report and anonymous case digests. There would be consistency and a build-up of 'case law'.

Those institutions persistently behaving badly would come to notice. A general university ombudsman would build up a body of expertise in the types of case that arise in universities and skills in this particular type of dispute resolution.

There are advantages and disadvantages to the ombudsman idea. An ombudsman can do only what is allowed by his or her remit, so the scope of the types of dispute he or she could look at would need to be sufficiently widely drawn to make it possible to bring in all the kinds of problem which now take students to courts or to the visitor. In any case, there would have to be 'political' will to set up such a system, particularly if it were to be done under statute.

Disputes involving universities may in certain limited circumstances already find themselves before the local government ombudsman. Investigation 94/C/2661, complaint against Cumbria County Council, was a complaint that an application for a discretionary award for tuition fees for a postgraduate course had not been properly considered in the absence of properly established criteria for measuring exceptional circumstances. The Council had an appeal procedure that allowed an appeal to be considered 'where there are exceptional circumstances relating to the specific course or to the appellant sufficient to justify a departure from the Council's approved policy'. The ombudsman referred to the 1993 *Guidance Note on Good Administrative Practice,* including the suggestion that there should be clear and relevant criteria that can be applied objectively (Axiom 4) and that reasons should be given for an adverse decision (Axiom 16).

The ombudsman concluded (27) that:

> The Council's system for considering each application for a discretionary grant on its merits without reference to any criteria, guidelines or previous decisions by Appeal Panels, lends itself to inconsistency and possible injustice.
>
> (28) The absence of a formal record of the reasons...means...that Panel members and officers advising them have no means of establishing that the reasoning behind their decisions has been fair and equitable. Nor has an unsuccessful appellant any means of knowing whether his or her appeal has been decided on proper grounds...

> (30) Whilst the Council's failure to establish criteria and guidelines for consideration of appeals and its failure to record reasons for decisions by Appeal Panels is maladministration.

So this kind of finding may be very helpful to a student complainant. But the scope for using it is very limited.

A system of independent review panels

Another possibility, favoured by the Second Nolan Report, is the establishment of a panel of independent arbitrators on whom universities could draw when their internal procedures have been exhausted. In September 1999 the then CVCP established a working party to prepare a report on the feasibility of a panel or panels of independent persons being set up to act as a forum for reviewing student complaints and complaints arising from public interest disclosure complaints in higher education institutions in the United Kingdom. The panel reported in a consultation document to which responses were invited in July 2000.

The powers of an independent review panel as discussed by the CVCP working party include determining whether the institution's internal investigation had been properly carried out and, if it was, determining whether the response was reasonable in all the circumstances.

The powers of the panel might also include making binding recommendations that:

- there be a further internal investigation;
- the institution reconsider the findings of the original investigation;
- there should be room for observations about lessons to be learnt;
- there should be opportunity for a ruling that the complainant was actuated by malice or another improper motive.

All this tends to assume that the panel would be arbitrating. Mediation would have the difference that the student and the university would both have to find the mediator acceptable, and that the university would not be bound by the decision. The National Mediation Centre in Swansea maintains a panel of mediators, some with educational or other relevant experience, from which a mediator or mediator can be recommended. That shows that such panel-systems can work. For schools, the DfEE has funded a charitable organization, the Shaftesbury Society, to offer conciliation (which is used in this context interchangeably with mediation) and also to offer training to local education authorities to help them identify circumstances where mediation may be appropriate. A provision of this sort could be extended to higher education.

The CVCP working party fights shy of requiring oral hearings. That is a pity. An oral hearing can make a substantial difference to the outcome and it would help to fulfil one of the most important functions of such an independent review, for it could help to reassure the complainant that there had (at last?) been a fair hearing.

The question of the composition of the panel or panels is not easily resolved. Speed and relevant expertise may be as important as independence to a student who needs to be free to get on with his or her life. Such working parties may be unduly optimistic about the effectiveness of choosing panel members for their seniority and especially for their experience in university administration. This may be 'experience' in the form of their allowing or even perpetrating exactly the kind of mistakes the panels will be reviewing. The panels would need access to legal advice. Members of the panels ought not to be chosen by nomination. Individuals ought to be able to apply.

Workload might be considerable in the first years, but might be expected to reduce as universities learned to handle student complaints and appeals better. In any case, this workload has to go somewhere and the courts are both an expensive place for it to end up and also an immensely time-consuming one.

A synthesis?

One of the possibilities being canvassed at the time of writing is a synthesis, in which the jurisdiction of visitors would be restricted by statutory change, so as to remove their powers to deal with complaints and appeals from individuals.(This could be, it is argued, done by one-line legislation.) Or visitors would be abolished altogether. The ombudsman option is coming into favour. A general, national university ombudsman would have the advantage over one for each university that it would be more easily perceived as independent by the complainant or appellant.

Experiments with a private-sector type of ombudsman, while the system evolves, would have the advantage of allowing time for the difficulties to be discovered and ironed out, perhaps with the intention of making statutory provision in due course. The difference is important. The autonomy of universities makes it difficult to force them to use any system of dispute resolution external to themselves, except the courts, where (with the visitor's jurisdiction shrunk or abolished) they would have no choice but to submit. A private-sector ombudsman could be ignored, although gradually public opinion might put pressure on a university that chose not to use the ombudsman system and the courts might be expected to look with disfavour on its refusal to do so. A statutory ombudsman would, in due course, have a good deal to recommend it although adequate provision would be expensive.

Under the ombudsman could stand something like the 'panel system' sketched above, putting into use the best of both schemes. The ombudsman would stand as a buffer between the appellant/complainant and would receive statements of complaint. Advice would be provided where appropriate (complaints being routed to a ring-fenced department for the purpose) to give complainants an opportunity to consider whether they would be satisfied with a letter to the university drawing its attention to unsatisfactory handling (rap over knuckles) or whether they want adjudication. The ombudsman would, as appropriate, route the complaint to persons with relevant expertise in the type of issue raised (members of the 'panels'). They would, following proper published procedures, hold hearings or inquiries as appropriate, and write a report.

The reports would build up into a body of material from which everyone could 'learn'. There could be tables for publication revealing the universities that were the subject of most complaints.

Alternative dispute resolution (ADR)

A further option is arbitration or mediation, which takes place not within a formal system especially set up for use by universities but as part of the provision under the Woolf reforms of 1999 for encouraging the use of alternatives to the courts. These differ in that arbitration involves the parties agreeing at the outset to be bound by the decision. Mediation requires no such undertaking but the procedural structures might be rather similar, beginning with a written statement of the problem, leading to a session in which both parties are present, a stage of testing the truth of what is alleged and another of exploring possible solutions, and a final session with everyone present. ADR is felt to be particularly helpful where there is an ongoing relationship to preserve; where a creative solution is needed not merely a financial settlement; and where the issues are complex.

The Lord Chancellor's Department published in May 2000 a summary of the responses to its consultation document: 'Alternative dispute resolution: a discussion paper' (unpublished, November, 1999). A key difficulty to emerge is whether arbitration should count as a form of alternative dispute resolution (presumably because of its binding character).

Student–staff overlap again

It is important not to lose sight of the fact that these routes to remedies for students overlap with those that are available to the staff of universities. Similar questions are being asked about the need for a better, fairer, more independent and more effective system for the resolution of staff complaints and grievances. This affects students too because a student complaint frequently involves members of staff, either as co-complainers or as those complained against, and it is very common for a complaint to overflow from one area to the other.

The courts

The reluctance of the courts to intervene

Even if it is accepted that there has been an injustice or a procedural impropriety, the courts may be reluctant to intervene. A long trail of cases may be read in the law reports where the student failed even though it was admitted that something had gone wrong that was the university's fault.

There are various reasons for this. The first is that an administrative decision has to be very unreasonable indeed before the courts feel justified in interfering with it, so the presumption is always that the university will get away with its mistakes. Universities know that and it can make them disinclined to be as open as they might be to student complaints. They can also believe that if they find in favour of the student they are somehow 'admitting fault'.

The second reason is that there is a long tradition that a university is a 'domestic' forum, so that what it does is no business of the courts. It is clearly unfair that students in all universities do not have the same rights and remedies in the courts, while so many continue to be subject to the jurisdiction of a visitor. The new universities are clearly public bodies and a student is in a stronger position there, but in an old university with a visitor, the courts have very little power to intervene in any way. It has been noted already that this could in principle be altered by statute, since the jurisdiction of the visitor in cases involving academic staff was altered in that way in the Education Reform Act 1988, s206. But at present the position for students in universities with visitors remains much the same as it has been for centuries.

Until the Further and Higher Education Act 1992, there was 'no uniformity in relation to the constitutional arrangements for the constitution and government of the universities'.[6] All universities predating the Act remained as they were, but from 1992, 'new universities could...be created under the procedures originally set out in the Education Reform Act 1988'.

The broad categories are:

1. Universities dating from before the Further and Higher Education Act 1992.
2. Higher education corporations established under the 1988 Education Reform Act, but after 1992.
3. Designated institutions under s129 of the 1988 Education Reform Act.
4. Higher Education Institutions maintained by the LEAs.

Categories 2 and 3 may be called 'universities' under s129 of the 1988 Act.

Some sections of the Education Reform Act 1988 provide statutory 'underpinning'. Section152(3) and (4) provides for the making of articles of government, which include 'procedures for admission, suspension and expulsion of students' and also the making of 'rules or bye-laws with respect to the conduct of staff and students'.

In the post-1992 universities (the former polytechnics) there is a statutory background, that is to say, the universities are set up under statutes of the realm and they do not have visitors, so the courts are more likely to

6 Hyams, O (1998) *Law of Education*, Sweet & Maxwell, London, p 497.

allow students from such institutions to apply for public law remedies and to entertain applications for leave for judicial review than they are if the student comes from an 'old' university, where there is a visitor. An example is the ruling that one new university was 'a body corporate by virtue of Chapter II of the Education Reform Act 1988. As a public institution discharging public functions, and having no visitor, it is subject to judicial review of its decision on the normal grounds'.[7]

In *Glynn v Keele University* [1971] 1 WLR 487, a student had been excluded from the University of Keele by direct action of the vice-chancellor, because he had gone about in the nude on the campus. Glynn did not dispute that he had done so, but he thought he ought to have been allowed to defend himself. He did not arrange to be present when the appeal was considered and he did not apply for a rehearing. The question was whether he was subsequently allowed to resort to the courts, for the University of Keele does have a visitor. It cannot be overemphasized that, this is an immensely difficult problem for the student who cannot, in effect, get 'outside' the domestic forum of his university for an independent decision about his complaint.

Public or private law

A third reason is that it can be unclear whether the student's complaint falls within the realm of private law (that is, where there is a legally binding relationship, such as contract, between two parties) or public law (where the overarching consideration is whether a public duty has been ignored). If a student chooses what the court takes to be the wrong route he or she may find the road blocked.

O'Reilly v Mackman [1983] 2 AC 237 at 285, took the view that it is, as a general rule:

> Contrary to public policy, and as such an abuse of the process of the court, to permit a person seeking to establish that a decision of a public authority infringed rights to which he was entitled to protection under public law to proceed by way of an ordinary action and by this means to evade the provisions of order 53.

---

7 *R v Manchester Metropolitan University, ex parte Nolan* [1994] ELR 380.

Other examples suggest that a student who tries the 'private law' route of bringing an action for breach of contract may find him- or herself before a judge who thinks that he or she ought to have sought judicial review. For example, if the student owes the university a debt for which the university is suing him or her, the right thing to do is to go to the small claims court to dispute it, or to try to pay by instalments if the university will agree to that.[8] But if the university has withheld examination results or graduation or refused to allow attendance at lectures, the right way forward may be to seek judicial review.[9]

In 1973 it was admitted that 'no one appears to have examined what the precise contractual relationship between [the students] and the university was'.[10] That is clearer now, especially in the light of *Clark v University of Lincolnshire and Humberside* [11] but there is still a good way to go before students can be confident that they are attempting the right route through the courts. One student, seeking review of the outcome of his PhD examination, tried court after court, and one cause of action after another, growing more and more desperate, until he found himself walking the pavements outside the University of North London handing out leaflets because that had become his only avenue of recourse.

Even if it is quite clear that the right way is the route of public law there is the problem that administrative law in the United Kingdom is weak and does not provide adequate remedies for the problem of maladministration. Universities are still largely their own masters and can do what they like in most respects, with the only real public accountability available being by way of media exposure and the possibility of withholding funds.

The regulations of a university are still likely to be regarded by the courts as its domestic laws. That presents a problem to the student who wants to complain that they have been broken. If they are not terms of his contract with the university and if they are not laws of the realm, or binding 'under' such statutory provision, the courts may well regard them as private in the same sort of way as the rules of a club or the arrangements within a family are entirely its own business. If the problem occurs in a university with a visitor the difficulty is even worse because, as we have seen, the

8 Maxwell, E (1999) The university contract, RAWS conference, Sheffield, 24 March.
9 Maxwell, E (1999) The university contract, RAWS conference, Sheffield, 24 March.
10 *Herring v Templeman* [1973] 3 All ER 569 at 585.
11 [2000] CA (*The Times*, 3 May 2000).

enforcement of the domestic laws becomes the visitor's business and the student has no remedy in the courts at all.

In a university with a visitor, students can find themselves outside the reach of a claim for negligence if domestic laws are carelessly followed and, as a consequence, a student fails to get his or her degree. In *Thorne v University of London* [1966] 2 WLR 1080 a student sought damages for the negligent marking of his examination papers. His writ was struck out as disclosing no reasonable cause of action, but only because questions about carrying into effect the regulations of the University were deemed to fall within the province of the visitor. Had there been no visitor he might conceivably have had a remedy through litigation.With these provisios, there are, then, several types of case a student may be able to bring when all else fails.

Judicial review

A recent case, *R v University of Cambridge, ex parte Persaud* (19 July 2000) is a good illustration of the way in which judicial review works. A student registered for a PhD was eventually de-registered by the University because it said that she had not been making progress. It was a long and complicated story that began when she said that her supervisor 'had involved her in collaboration without her knowledge and was more interested in using her work for his own purposes'. There were more supervision problems with a series of supervisors. The student kept failing to go to the laboratory to work and failing to keep in contact with her supervisor. The University did, in fact, give her a lot of extra chances. She sought judicial review of the University's decision. If she had succeeded the court could have quashed the decision.and the University would then either have had to take it again in such a way that the court could not quarrel with it, or to reinstate her.

Her barrister argued several points, all raising questions of proper procedure, for the court could not make a decision about the quality of her work; that was not its job. The first was that the decision had been taken unfairly. The university had not told her of the existence or identity of the senior member of the faculty who had provided an opinion on reports of her work and it had refused to disclose to her the reports that had been made on her so that she could comment on them. She therefore had no opportunity to know whether this was someone who had been prejudiced against her or to discuss the accuracy of the comments. That the judge did not accept the unfairness is a matter of some concern because, in a disciplinary case, everyone has a right to know of accusations and to be allowed an opportunity to answer them, and there should, in that arena, be no such thing as an 'anonymous' judgmental comment. On the other hand, what was being made here was partly an academic judgment and Mr Justice Maurice Kay went that way in this case.

The second ground of the challenge by judicial review was that 'there was a failure to give the Applicant adequate, proper and intelligible reasons' for the decision to remove her name from the register of graduate students. But some reasons had been given and the judge said that they were enough. The third ground was that there was a 'fetter of discretion' – in other words that pre-existing policies had been applied without regard to the circumstances of the particular case. These were the policies not to disclose reports and a policy that reinstatement could only be considered if the student had completed the project for which she was registered. Because the student had actually been given many extra chances and allowed to remain on the register for more years than usual, this ground for challenge also failed. Then there was a challenge that there had been 'unlawful delegation' – that is, that the discretion had been made not by the proper authority but by someone whose opinion had been asked, and a challenge that the degree committee had acted beyond its powers in appointing a senior academic to provide a report. (Permission has now been given for appeal.)

These are the kinds of matters that can be argued in judicial review cases. From a student's point of view they are highly technical and abstract aspects of what has actually happened.

Judicial review is designed to promote good public administration. Until and unless a public sector ombudsman system extends its remit to universities, this is the best way to challenge administrative decisions. Judicial review is a 'public law' remedy, which can be attempted in the first instance only if the university has no visitor and if the matter at issue is a 'public law' issue over which the university was acting as a public body.

The time limit for seeking judicial review is three months, but it is important to act promptly because the courts will hold any delay against the applicant. Legal advice needs to be obtained quickly from a solicitor specializing in education law.

Judicial review takes place in two stages. The first involves obtaining permission, and the second the full hearing. Judicial review has to be applied for within three months of the decision the student wants to complain about and as promptly as possible but, except in a genuine emergency, it may take up to a year to reach a full hearing.

If a judicial review succeeds, the High Court can do three main things. It can quash the decision and require the university to take it again (*quashing order*). It can order the university to do something (*mandatory order*). It can prohibit it from doing something. It cannot award damages. And the kinds of things it will interfere with do not include requiring the university to give a student a degree or a particular class of degree. The university can get round what is required of it by putting right its procedural mistakes, taking the decision again, and coming to the same conclusion.

But judicial review is not the weak remedy that this suggests. It is a high-profile business, with the media frequently taking an interest. Universities regard it with some anxiety and may be prompted to put things right for themselves if the student obtains leave. There can be an injunction. Judicial review is, however, a specialist area of the law and it may be an expensive way to go to court unless the student can get legal aid.

The Human Rights Act 1998

The Human Rights Act will not create a new cause of action, or basis on which a case can be brought in the first instance. It will have to be cited in one of the types of case that can already be brought.

The rights under the European Convention on Human Rights exist primarily against the state, and public authorities and bodies exercising public power. Universities will probably count under that heading for this purpose. This is important because if something is held to be *merely* a private, contractual matter, a student may not be able to make use of the Human Rights Act in litigation.

Article 6 has already generated more case law in a European context than any other Convention right. It guarantees due process of law:

> In the determination of his civil rights and obligations or of any criminal charge against him, everyone is entitled to a fair and public hearing within a reasonable time by an independent and impartial tribunal established by law.

The right to a fair trial applies to many administrative decisions that have been held to involve 'civil rights and obligations'. It is widely agreed that the visitor system is unlikely to meet the requirements of Article 6, at least as it is at present constituted. In the 'new' universities, which do not have visitors, there is going to be the difficulty that, even though the courts can provide a forum in which a trial is 'independent', it is unusual for a court to be willing to feel itself able to look at the merits of the case, and it will never address questions of academic judgement.

Various other Articles may affect a university's duties. Under the first Protocol, Article 2, there is a right to education that may give rise to cases about access and admissions policies. Article 8 protects the right to privacy. If a university makes checks on e-mails it may be infringing that right. Article 9 protects the right to freedom of thought, conscience and religion. Article 10 protects the right to freedom of expression. For students, these are in part protected by the Education Act 1986, s43. Article 14 gives a right to freedom from discrimination, going wider than the present provisions against sexual, racial and disability discrimination and covering discrimination because of any 'status' that makes a person different from others. The protection of Article 2 against inhuman or degrading treatment is not likely to be applicable in the situations that arise in universities but it would be wise for them not to be too complacent on this point. Students are occasionally subjected to oral abuse by members of staff, which could be held to fall into this area.

Universities will have to act consistently with Convention rights and when deciding issues affecting individuals universities shall have to be prepared to consider arguments based on those rights. In determining the propriety of any restrictions on the Convention rights it has to be asked whether the proposed restriction on a Convention right is proportional to the purpose that the restriction serves ('proportionality'). In *Handyside v UK*, the doctrine of the margin of appreciation was developed. It was designed to allow national mechanisms a degree of flexibility when being assessed by an international system of adjudication. In other words, more than one legitimate course of action may be open in a given state.

Liberty, in *Getting it Right* (November, 1998) points out that the law must be adequately accessible. Liberty also notes that a norm cannot be regarded as a 'law' unless it is formulated with sufficient precision to enable the citizen to regulate his or her conduct. They say that 'codes of practice or internal guidance are very unlikely to meet the requirements of certainty'.

Contract

Cases about breach of contract may also be blocked by the existence of a visitor. That is now not so clear as it was, and the *Times Higher Education Supplement* of 6 August 1999 carried a front-page article on a survey by Tim Birtwhistle of the lack of awareness among university administrators that there *is* now a contract with students. Again and again, in the cases described in this book, there have been problems arising from the lack of clarity of institutions about the implications of the contractual relationship.

The position is a great deal clearer in the light of *Clark v University of Lincolnshire and Humberside* (19 April 2000). It was held that the new universities, which are statutory corporations, and perhaps Oxford and Cambridge, which are civil corporations, have 'the ordinary attributes of legal personality and a capacity to enter into contracts'. They are also arguably public bodies, so there then arises a question of whether a litigant ought to follow a public law route, in other words, to seek judicial review, rather than to sue in contract. This can be an important consideration. It is known for a university to appear in a court in a private law case and argue that the case ought to have been brought by way of judicial review and to appear in a judicial review application and argue that the case ought to have been brought in contract. There are precedents both ways.[12] It is important because of the considerable difference in time limits. The courts want to avoid allowing someone who has been very slow in seeking judicial review being able to make use of the six-year time limit for contract.

An increasingly common scene is the failure to provide what has been promised or implied in the contract. The course may not be run at all if insufficient students are accepted. One student who applied for a specialist art course complained that when this happened she was not informed, but was allowed to incur expense in giving up her job, making arrangements to begin the course, moving and organising finance. Not until five days before the course was due to begin did she hear from the college, by a message left on her answerphone, that the course was to be cancelled.

12 *Cocks v Thanet District Council* [1983] 2 AC 287 held that if private law rights depended on prior public law decisions they must ordinarily be litigated by judicial review. But in *Wandsworth LBC v Winder* [1985] AC 461 and *Roy v Kensington, Chelsea and Westminster Family Practitioners Committee* [1992] 1 AC 624 it was held that was not necessarily the case. In *Clark* it was found to be important that the public law element was not dominant.

Specialist courses are especially vulnerable to this sort of thing. A special case of the promise of specialist provision is supervision for a PhD. Another student came to a university to study for a PhD on the undertaking that he would have a particular named supervisor. When he moved with his family from Dubai he learned that the supervisor had moved to another university many hundreds of miles away. Indeed he could not begin his course because he was not even given access to the university's research facilities. This case exemplifies a situation that can be very difficult for a university because, at the level of doctoral research, the supervision needed is very specialized. This university could have informed the student immediately the prospective supervisor decided to move and it appears to have falsified its own records to suggest that he had withdrawn from the course at an early date; if it did so it compounded its breach of contract.

Another student wanted to take a course in international disaster engineering and management, which the college claimed was unique. It turned out that the staff were not qualified or experienced in this area. Sent to gain experience at a local fire station, the students discovered that the university had failed to arrange the necessary health and safety insurance. The university told the students that 'it is not unusual in the launch of a new programme of study for there to be teething troubles'. But this was these students' only chance to take the course.

Then there are courses whose purpose is to equip students for professional qualifications or provide them with a basis for professional recognition. The institution has a duty to meet such requirements. A student studying for a diploma in social work at a college of higher and further education was given oral assurances that the diploma course on which he was embarking would meet the requirements of the Central Council for Education and Training in Social Work. Those requirements must at least have included providing proper supervision so that the student could identify weak areas of his work, enabling the student to gain knowledge about the legislative framework and statutory duties and powers of social work agencies, arranging appropriate placements. The student complained that the college had failed him at all these points.

Some courses promise to equip students with practical skills. A course for a higher national diploma in vehicle restoration and conservation technology was offered by a college. The course did not begin at all until four months beyond the promised starting date. The 'workshop' was a disused classroom with plastic flooring in which it was obviously impossible to practise welding.

Some courses promise combinations of subjects. A student was accepted by a university for a degree in computing and modern languages. Both she and the university seem to have understood that this was a combined honours course. But the two departments involved saw it differently and they apparently did not liaise. This became a major difficulty in the third year when the student was to be sent to Spain to gain experience of computing in that country. A document supplied by the university stated that: 'It is hoped that the majority of students will be placed in an organisational environment where they undertake professional level computer work'. The student was not helped to find her placement and while other students doing only Spanish were able to get grants from Erasmus for the study year abroad, this student was not told of that possibility and seems to have been treated as a computing student doing a little Spanish. It was not until late in her third year that the student was told that there was 'no officially approved Combined Honours in computing and languages'. The degree the student eventually obtained was in 'computing studies' alone. She was legally advised that the degree she was awarded was not the one contracted for. In that and other respects, the university had not delivered on its promise.

Tort: negligence

A university has both a duty of care towards a student and a duty to maintain reasonable professional standards. It offers a student education of a professional standard appropriate to its degree-awarding powers. It entrusts the 'delivery' of that education to its employees or to others by some formal arrangement such as franchising. If they carelessly do not 'deliver the goods', or not to an acceptable standard, there may be grounds to sue for negligence.

The individuals who 'failed to deliver', as well as the institution, may be personally liable. The more senior the individual the higher the professional standard that he or she will have been expected to meet.

This can be quite important 'tactically' for the student because it is common for employees of a university to try to sit it out or to hide behind the institution, in the confidence that they will never be called to account personally. That confidence may be misplaced.

If a student wants to establish the 'tort' of negligence, a first main requirement is that there should be a relationship of sufficient proximity[13] between the person damaged by the alleged negligence and the person or body whose fault it was. That relationship undoubtedly exists between a student and a university.

X (Minors) v Bedfordshire County Council [1995] 2 AC 633 and *Barrett v Enfield LBC* [1999] 3 All ER, established that there is a duty to exercise reasonable professional skills. The principle here covers 'operational' negligence in the exercise of professional responsibilities.

The argument that there is a *vicarious* liability may be helpful. That means that the university or college can be sued for the negligence of its academic or other employees. *X (Minors) v Bedfordshire County Council* [1995] 2 AC 633 and *Barrett v Enfield LBC* [1999] 3 All ER, established the principle that failure by the local authority, acting through its social workers and others, to safeguard the welfare of a child it had taken into its care, gives rise to liability. The direct duty of care was ruled out on public policy grounds, because it would expose local authorities to financial risk from a flood of damages claims with no reasonable prospect of success.[14] It was argued that 'vicarious liability' would afford sufficient remedy, where it was shown that the local authority had offered a service that its agents had failed to provide. For those responsible for teachers in breach of a duty of care may be vicariously liable for their negligence, *Hippolyte v London Borough of Bexley* [1995] PIQR 309, CA. In *Gower v London Borough of Bromley, The Times*, 28 October 1999 (CA) it was held that teachers are under a duty to exercise reasonable skill in responding to the educational needs of their pupils, and that the local authority could be vicariously liable for breach of that duty.[15]

In *Barrett v Enfield London Borough Council* [1999] 3 All ER 193 HL at 198 it was held that 'social workers dealing with sex abuse cases cannot be expected to be always looking over their shoulders at their own liability in negligence'. In *Phelps v London Borough of Hillingdon* [1999] 1 All ER, too,

13 In determining whether there is an arguable duty of care the court should have regard to the threefold *Caparo v Dickman* test of foreseeability, proximity and 'fair, just and reasonable'. As to 'fair, just and reasonable', *Osman v UK* (1998) 5 BHRC 293 establishes that assessment can normally only properly be made after full consideration of the evidence and circumstances at trial.

14 The European Court of Human Rights in *Osman v UK* (1998) 5 BHRC 293 held that the public policy exclusion of negligence actions might violate Article 6 (1) of the European Convention on Human Rights.

15 See too *Phelps v London Borough of Hillingdon* [1998] 1 ELR 38.

there was reluctance to award compensation to a dyslexic child whose problems had not been recognized by the educational psychologist who should have assessed him. This appears to overturn an earlier decision by the House of Lords, that 'a school which accepts a pupil assumes responsibility not only for his physical well-being but also for his educational needs' (*X v Bedfordshire* [1995] 3 All ER 353 at 395 and [1995] 2 AC 633 at 763, per Lord Browne-Wilkinson).

The House of Lords has recently decided in the *Phelps* series of cases that negligence claims can properly be brought against teachers and other professionals in education. This is important because it makes it more likely that the staff of universities can be brought into the frame individually and not allowed to 'hide behind' the institution in ways that affect a student and cause loss. (*Phelps v Hillingdon, Gower v Bromley and others*, House of Lords, 27 July 2000.) It was held that a person exercising a particular skill or profession may owe a duty of care in the performance of it to people who can be foreseen to be at risk of loss, damage or injury if due skill and care are not exercised. The standard to be applied was a reasonable professional standard. Direct liability of the employer was also not ruled out where there was operational negligence, but that has yet to be established in a series of further cases before the House of Lords. Connected, too, is *Michael Hyde and Associates v JD Williams & Co Ltd, The Times*, 4 August 2000, in which Sedley LJ said 'that professional negligence meant falling below a proper standard of competence'.

The rules for whoever is preparing the case (see Civil Procedure Rules 35) would expect an expert giving evidence to be clear about the facts on which he or she is relying, those that tell both for and against his or her view, the published authorities that he or she is using, the exact respects in which specific actions fell below the standard of a professionally reasonably competent person, and the range of professional opinion on these points that has to be taken into consideration (*Bolam v Friern Hospital Management Committee* [1957] 2 All ER 118).

It will still be difficult to prove the link between the professional negligence and the consequence to the student, however, and to quantify the loss. In *Blamire v South Cumbria Health Authority* (1993) PIQR QI, the basis for the calculation of damages was the loss of opportunity to earn at a higher rate. That might be argued by a dyslexic student where the university failed to identify and provide for his or her needs.

The Sun carried a headline on 19 November 1999: 'Cleaner bins 149 exam papers.' A cleaner had accidentally thrown away the unmarked examination papers of students sitting for a qualification from the Institute of Linguists. That was arguably negligence – not, perhaps, 'professional negligence' but still a careless mistake that had caused the students' loss. As one of them was quoted as saying: 'We've got to go through the exam stress all over again.' Here, too, there might be something that the courts can do.

Discrimination

The Sex Discrimination Act 1975, s77(3) and the Race Relations Act 1976, s72(3) would appear to give a student a potential cause of action.[16] The Disability Discrimination Act 1995 does not make specific provision for students and, although the extension of its provisions to educational establishments is likely to be completed soon, it is not in place yet.

Student action checklist

- ✔ Ask the university for a list of all the internal 'avenues of recourse' it provides.
- ✔ Find out about time limits and the order in which such internal procedures have to be used.
- ✔ Make sure you go through all these stages before considering going outside the university, but keep an eye on the statutory time limits for putting claims in to the courts. You are allowed three months to put in an application for judicial review, but you should not delay as long as that if you can avoid it. In judicial review proceedings the courts expect applications to be put in promptly. You must bring a claim for personal injury within three years. You must bring a claim arising out of breach of contract and negligence within six years.
- ✔ If you need legal advice try the students' union first, so as to get free legal advice in that way if you can. Alternatively, if, like most students, you have a low income, you will be entitled to up to two hours' free

16 'A term in a contract which purports to exclude or limit any provision of the Act...is unenforceable by any person in whose favour the term would operate.'

advice and assistance under the 'legal help and help at court' scheme provided by the Legal Services Commission. If you are not eligible for that scheme, ask for a fixed fee interview with a solicitor.

- ✔ If you go to a solicitor check that you have approached one with specialist knowledge. A general solicitor or a specialist in family or employment law may not have the knowledge to give you reliable advice. Legal advice is expensive and it is important to spend the money on the best advice you can get.
- ✔ Get the solicitor to try writing a warning letter or suggest alternative dispute resolution as a means of avoiding a court case.
- ✔ Do not begin legal action unless you are prepared for a very long and stressful struggle. Universities will usually fight hard and ruthlessly against their own students once the matter reaches the courts. They have a great deal more money than the student and if the student loses the university may try to recover enormous costs against the student.
- ✔ Universities dislike damage to their reputations. The media can be used as a 'pressure group' to encourage the university to settle with you but that should be a last resort because you will have no control over the way they tell the story.

11

The student whistleblower and the university's response to criticism

Critical speaking

Students with a complaint often want to point to failings in the university's conduct of its affairs that affect other students beside themselves. They may want to point to what seems to them to be misconduct in a scientific research project. Or they may simply have constructive suggestions to make.

There is a natural reluctance to take the risk of speaking out because of the fear of consequences if the university resents the criticism. Students are in a vulnerable position when they do not yet have their degrees and when they will depend on referees from the university to launch their careers. The law is not helpful to students here. The student whistleblower is not protected by the Public Interest Disclosure Act from the reprisals that may follow, because it is an *employment* protection, designed to protect conscientious whistleblowers from losing their jobs. The Education Reform Act 1988, s202, protects a limited category of permanent academic staff against being put in jeopardy of losing their jobs or privileges at their institution for exercising an 'academic' freedom of speech. Even for them, however, it is not yet clear whether this covers criticism of the running of the institution. Again it is an employment protection issue.

It looks as though, to enjoy a similar protection, students would have to have it written into their 'contracts' with the university. There is one possible existing protection: The Education (No 2) Act 1986, s43 provides that:

> (1) Every individual and body of persons concerned in the government of any establishment to which this section applies shall take such steps as are reasonably practical to ensure that freedom of speech within the law is secured for members, students and employees of the establishment and for visiting speakers.

In the framing of the 1986 Act the issue was the creation and preservation of an environment on university campuses where individuals could speak freely without fear of being forcibly prevented. The need for legislation had been created by a series of episodes in which militant students had sought to prevent invited speakers from delivering their addresses. An attempt by dissidents at the London School of Economics to prevent Sir Keith Joseph speaking there was outwitted by action on the part of the director, who issued a fresh invitation and ensured that the speaker was allowed to speak.[1]

Another episode involved censorship by those in charge of an institution. At the University of Bristol, Tony Benn was asked to speak at an Open Day on 14 July 1979. There was confusion about the title to which he had agreed. Posters were put up carrying a title that gave offence to some. The Dean of the School of Education, Professor Boris Ford, approached the vice-chancellor, Alec Merrison, and the lecture was cancelled.

On 15 February 1986 there was a debate in the House of Lords on the avoidance of 'politicization in education'.[2] Baroness Cox made a long speech on two issues which she conjoined in a paradoxical manner under 'the politicization of education'. On the one hand, she argued, it was important to ensure that 'the principle of freedom of speech in universities, colleges and schools' was protected. 'Freedom of speech,' she said, 'is a touchstone of a free society and is essential for the pursuit of truth and knowledge which lies at the heart of education as we know it.' She argued that this was being violated by a form of censorship consisting of 'physical and verbal attacks' on visiting speakers ('sometimes Ministers of State'). She called for 'the guardians of our academies' to 'make freedom of speech their overriding commitment, however unpalatable the views of the speaker may be to them or to their militant students'. She called for disciplining of the disrupters.

---

1 This is a good example of the need to strike a balance between two freedoms.

2 HL Deb 1986, vol 470, 1138.

On the other hand, she argued, it was important to prevent 'the politicization of teaching and curricula'. She gave examples of teaching in schools that carried political messages, for example 'an anti-racist maths lesson'. She had in mind what she described as a 'view of education as part of the revolutionary struggle'. These conflicting messages, that (within the law) in the educational arena one must be able to say what one pleases, and that certain types of speech ought to be banned, she attempted to draw together in one somewhat breathless sentence: 'Education in a free society should enshrine the principles of freedom of speech, freedom to pursue the truth and freedom to develop views and interests *not predetermined by the political commitments of local authorities or of teachers*.'[3] It was the second of the Baroness's themes that the other speakers took up, and no one pointed to the inherent contradiction in what she had said.[4]

There were further Questions and Answers in the House of Commons on 18 February 1986. John Carlisle had himself been the object of what the Prime Minister, sympathizing with him, called 'nasty incidents'. 'I believe and hope that the whole House agrees that upholding freedom of speech in our institutions of higher education is vital...Freedom of speech consists of being able to say things that are not acceptable to everyone.'[5] On 4 March 1986 there was a question about the guidelines issued by the CVCP on 'freedom of speech and lawful assembly'. The answer stressed that the CVCP guidelines 'reiterate the universities' unequivocal and forthright support for freedom of speech'.[6]

The 1986 Act thought in terms of 'lawful assembly'. It provided for a protected environment for academic freedom of speech *within* the institution. There, anyone may in principle enjoy that right. Because of the public concern over the treatment of a number of visiting speakers, the relationships in which it is envisaged that speaker may stand to institution are drafted so as to comprehend as wide a range as possible, even the most casual visitor, for example a visiting speaker present for an hour or two only is included. Not only academic staff or academic topics are protected, but,

---

3 HL Deb 1986, Vol 470, 1138–46.

4 The Government issued a Green Paper on The Treatment of Politically Controversial Issues in Schools and Colleges [1986] PL 331.

5 HC Deb, 8 February 1986, Vol 93, 1184.

6 HC Deb, 4 March 1986, Vol 94, 111. Another question on 18 March took a similar line, 159. At 308w there was a written answer on the protection of freedom of speech in polytechnics.

apparently, remarks made by, for example, porters and cleaners, and on any subject at all.

It is all about the 'environment'. The defining consideration is whether the speech takes place within the institution, apparently in the physical sense of 'on the premises'. That is, paradoxically, confirmed by the additional provision that if a students' union happens to occupy 'premises which are not premises of the establishment in connection with which the union is constituted', it shall be included as though it did. That localization of the protection is made explicit in s43 (2):

> The duty imposed by subsection (1) above includes (in particular) the duty to ensure, so far as is reasonably practicable, that *the use of any premises of the establishment* is not denied to any individual or body of persons on any grounds connected with -
> (a) the beliefs or views of that individual or of any member of that body; or
> (b) the policy or objectives of that body [emphasis added].

Again, (a) and (b) are not confined to academic issues.

The Act further provides for each 'establishment' to 'issue and keep up to date a code of practice' for the conduct of 'meetings' or 'activities' *on the premises*. There is a clear understanding in the Act that free speech protections of this type are appropriate only to tertiary education. Universities and establishments of further education maintained by local education authorities are specified. Section 44 of the same Act covers separately protections against the second of Baroness Cox's concerns, political indoctrination in schools.

The paradox remains unresolved. A student in a final summer term in a school has a right to be protected from politically partisan influence, presumably because he or she still has a tender young mind, whereas the same student having moved on in the subsequent term to a university or college of further education must be allowed to say and hear anything that is said within the law, and his or her new teachers may (apparently) be as biased as they please. There is a deep incoherence here, which reflects the 'reactive' character of this legislation.

It is not clear what would be the remedy if rights under this Act were violated. In *R v University College, London, ex parte Ursula Rineker* [1995] ELR 213 Sedley J was 'prepared to accept that s43 is justiciable by judicial review in an appropriate case. It does not appear to create private rights, which can readily be assured by other means'. But that was a staff case, not a student case.

Public interest disclosure and students

The best way forward for students in the short term is for universities voluntarily to include protections for students in their codes under the Public Interest Disclosure Act or codes on misconduct in research. Oxford has done so:

> The University expects...staff and students...to observe the highest standards in the conduct of their research...suspicions reported in confidence and in good faith will not lead to disciplinary proceedings against the person making the complaint.[7]

The Nolan Committee, in its second report, stated (Recommendation 7):

> Institutions of higher and further education should make it clear that the institution permits staff to speak freely and without being subject to disciplinary sanctions or victimisation about academic standards and related matters, provided they do so lawfully, without malice, and in the public interest.

The CVCP guidelines (1999) on the Public Interest Disclosure Act are designed to include students and members of governing bodies as well as staff. The CVCP guidelines promise that 'no detrimental action of any kind will be taken under this procedure against a person within the institution making a complaint of a nature described above, provided it is done without malice and in good faith, reasonably believing it to be true'.

The difficulty with this is that only formal disciplinary action can realistically be prevented. Reprisals take many forms, as students fear.

One warning note needs to be sounded. Freedom of speech may cover far more than the freedom to speak up about the conduct of the institution. Freedom of speech is not absolute. There are forms of speech which the law outlaws, such as speech inciting to racial hatred or to violence or to disruption of public order. A student cannot claim an 'academic' right of freedom of speech in such circumstances. Academic freedom of speech is a

7 *Oxford University Gazette Supplement* (3) to 4517, 30 June 1999.

freedom 'within the law' (cf s202 of the Education Reform Act 1988). Outside the law, as King's College, London makes clear in its rules, is 'distributing or publishing of a poster, notice, sign or any publication (including electronically circulated material) which is threatening, abusive, insulting or is otherwise illegal or makes others fear violence'.

It is also important for students to be careful in making use of a university's e-mail address in connection with such 'speech', either by using it to circulate e-mails containing unlawful speech or by inviting recipients of publicity material to respond to a university e-mail address. That may constitute misuse of university property, and be an internal disciplinary offence in its own right.

The university's response to criticism

'Complaints management in Higher Education' ran the advertisement for a course operated by Capita Business Services on 14 May 1999: 'The student is now seen as a "client" who demands high levels of service. As a result complaints and appeals in Higher education have significantly increased. Failure to manage complaints comprehensively could cause problems for your organisation.'

There was a suggestion that good complaints 'management' could lead to 'quality improvements' but the leading idea seemed to be that complaints are likely to cause trouble, rather than that student needs ought to be coming first with the university. That makes it difficult for universities to create a climate of expectation, which ought to be universal, that there will be an attempt at problem solving and reconciliation. Friendly relations can be re-established; a middle way can be found, if there is goodwill. At present that is rarely the pattern.

It was remarked a generation ago that 'higher administrators are not known to be favourable to having their goals changed by subordinates',[8] and students are the most subordinate of all in a university. A university will

8 Weinstein, D (1979) *Bureaucratic Opposition: Challenging abuses at the workplace*, Pergamon, New York, p 88.

tend to react by defending its own conduct if it is criticized.[9] It will not usually admit fault and if it puts things right it is likely to try to do so rather quietly. Yet students often say that they want to be able to feel that something has been learned from what has happened to them, and it can transform a situation for the student complainant to see that it has. Failures to devise and insist on patterns of conduct of affairs that give a fair hearing in a reasonable time to a student (or a member of staff) with a problem, with minds open to the possibility that the university may be at fault, may in the end lead to intervention.

When something goes wrong in a university, especially in its financial management or in the area of health and safety, it may find itself being 'visited' by regulatory bodies, such as the Health and Safety Executive, the Environment Agency, the Data Protection Registrar, the Trading Standards or Environmental Health Department of the local authority. Students can report their concerns directly to these regulators if they have tried to get the university to listen and nothing has been done.

Media interest increases pressure where a university is resistant to tackling a problem or dealing with a complaint. This can be devastating for an institution without large resources and an established position. Even a richer and older university, with a press office and used to press comment, can be made to face up to the need to explain itself very publicly.

One of the administrative effects of a 'public' crisis is that the administration is put under great strain, managers become demoralized and distracted, and there is what is known as 'opportunity cost', that is, resources have to be taken from other tasks and concentrated upon dealing with the crisis. It is much better if this is avoided, but it is, in the end, the complainant's only answer to institutional intransigence and administrative delay.

The end of the road can take the form of audit by a Higher Education Funding Council, and then by the National Audit Office, with public hearings and adverse reports, going on perhaps to an investigation by the Public Accounts Committee. Maladministration is not easy to show, or to get action on, given the current state of the law, but there have been cases

9 'Once a political process has been unleashed in a bureaucracy the first concerns of the authorities are to contain it within the organization, reassert the chain of command, and refurbish the administrative myth. They may also attempt to correct the abuses, but they will try to do so without admitting that there are abuses.' Weinstein, D (1979) *Bureaucratic Opposition: Challenging abuses at the workplace,* Pergamon, New York, p 108.

concerning the *way* things have been handled. Lord Donaldson said in *R v Local Commissioner for Administration, ex parte Eastleigh Borough Council* [1998] 1 QB 855 at 863 that administration and maladministration have nothing to do with the reasonableness of the decision itself. Another possible charge is 'misfeasance in public office' (*Three Rivers DC v Bank of England* [1999] EuLR 211).

Student action checklist

- ✔ The best place to start with the raising of a concern 'in the public interest' is with the statutory or other bodies listed in this book. Their telephone numbers can be found through directory enquiries. It is also a good idea to copy letters to your local MP and to the Secretary of State for Education.
- ✔ Going to the media is a last resort. The media may want to put a 'spin' on the story that you are not happy with and you will not be able to prevent that. You may also become 'notorious', and that could damage your future career prospects.

Conclusion

This may appear an unedifying tale, and indeed anyone intimate with the running of universities and the ways in which they handle complaints and appeals and disputes with their students and staff would find it hard not to be aware that a great culture-change is needed. Universities are complex societies and not easy to run well and they do not have a good record for seeing their way clearly through the ordering of priorities. From a student's-eye view that is alarming, for the individual student is in a weak and precarious position.

Hundreds, perhaps thousands, of lives full of promise are being cut short professionally by incompetence in the administration of universities and colleges. Students coming straight from school, in particular, are too innocent and too young to stand a chance of getting their complaints heard and sensibly addressed without help. The universities and colleges themselves ought to be giving them that help. The evidence before the authors, from dealing with dozens of cases, is that they are not doing so, or at least not regularly and routinely doing so.

The fault lies for the most part not in lack of goodwill, but in lack of training, expertise and sheer awareness of the obligations upon providers of higher education, and lack of funding to enable universities to put their house in order in this area. We hope that administrators and academics as well as students will read this book and that, consequently, fewer cases will linger unaddressed or badly handled, and unresolved, until they begin to consume the institution's time and money and destroy its reputation.

The change needed is not in the direction of further government intervention or state control. It is essential that universities retain a degree of autonomy or they cannot fulfil their traditional purposes of fostering education, learning and research. They cannot stand up to governments if they are in the hands of politicians or insist on truth and accuracy and independence in research if they can be bought or intimidated. But the sort of change called for in this book is not like that. It asks only for a degree of humility and common sense, a willingness to admit to error and lapses of procedural fairness when they occur and goodwill to put things right for the sake of students whose futures are at stake.

Appendix: student action checklist – general points

The 'ordinary student' ought to be able to expect certain things. This is a student checklist of golden rules for guidance as to what that means. If you find you are being treated differently the list also contains some general practical advice, ground rules, and suggestions for further steps to take if problems persist.

Being treated as an 'ordinary student' should expect to be treated is not a privilege but a fundamental right. Standing up for good standards can help others as well as you.

- ✔ Ask for copies of all the university's procedures affecting students. These should include not only complaints and discipline procedures but also codes of practice on such matters as harassment, discrimination (sexual, racial and disability), public interest disclosure, plagiarism, misconduct with regard to research.
- ✔ Find out who the university expects you to go to if you have any problems. Is there a 'university ombudsman' in your university? Is there a counselling service? Are any members of staff (such as tutors) given special responsibilities for troubleshooting? Who are the Students' Union officers? It should be possible for the university to hand you a list of names, telephone numbers and e-mail addresses if you ask.
- ✔ Ask which of these are advisors and which can take a complaint forward through the university's procedures if necessary.

If anything happens to you as a student that begins to cause you concern, keep the following rules carefully from the beginning. This does not mean that you are being mistrustful of the university's good intentions about handling student complaints, but you cannot take it for granted that a complaint is going to be resolved easily and it is important to be prepared if it turns out that it will be a long, drawn-out process. That often happens.

- ✔ Keep records. Write down and keep a detailed note of any conversations or meetings concerning the complaint, whom they were with and which aspect of the problem was discussed. Record the date. Do this for events 'within' the area of the complaint and also (in a separate file) for events that occur when you begin to try to raise the complaint through the university's procedures. Concentration on the specific and particular, including exactly what was said, can be very important if a student meets attempts to dismiss the complaint as a 'wild accusation'.
- ✔ Print out and keep all e-mails.
- ✔ Be particularly careful not to use e-mail as a way to let off steam. E-mails in connection with your complaint should be as carefully written as a letter. The university can access them if it chooses, even if you do not put them into the file of documents yourself.
- ✔ Letters written by the student should be as short as possible and concentrate on the point at issue. It is a good idea to number the points because that makes it easier to notice when expressions of distress are beginning to creep in. Take those out before you send the letter. The complaint is much stronger and more likely to succeed if it keeps to specific omissions or actions. You should, however, explain briefly any loss or damage that you have suffered.
- ✔ Obtain legal advice. If a problem is not resolved at once when you raise it with someone in authority it is important to obtain legal advice at an early stage. Go to a solicitor who has experience of judicial review, employment or 'education' work. Not all firms of solicitors have the correct sort of expertise. This is not the same as planning to go to court but it will help to ensure that mistakes are not made that could 'damage' the case later on if you do have to go to court. A letter from a solicitor might also be helpful in bringing things to a quick resolution.
- ✔ The majority of students will be eligible for up to two hours of free advice under the Legal Help Scheme because of their low income. The student should ask in advance whether that will be possible and how much it will cost.

Step-by-step points when you have to make a formal complaint

- ✔ Ask for the university's written code of conduct or guidelines or procedure for dealing with the kind of complaint you need to make.
- ✔ If there is no code or procedure insist that a procedure be agreed before the complaint is looked into. It is notoriously difficult to make universities keep their own rules and fairness will be even more difficult to ensure when the rules have to be made up on the spot.
- ✔ Separate the issues in your mind. A complaint can have a number of elements in it and each of them may need to be addressed separately under a different procedure. You will be much more effective if you 'ride the right horse at the right fence'. It is also usually a good idea not to try to tackle every aspect of a problem but to single out what really matters and concentrate on that.
- ✔ You may need advice and an opportunity to talk things through to enable you to get the problem under control in this way. If you go for advice to a member of staff, remember that that person is not allowed under the rules of natural justice to play any part in the consideration of your complaint or appeal later on unless you consent. That protects you, so that you can speak freely without fear of what you say being 'used against' you when the complaint is formally considered.
- ✔ The university may well have to be reminded of this rule. It is very common for a member of staff to whom a student has entrusted confidences to go and talk to colleagues, perhaps in an attempt to be helpful, but with disastrous results for the possibility of a 'fair trial' of the issues.
- ✔ Always keep a record on paper of each step you take. If you make a request for extra time in an examination because you are dyslexic, for example, write down the date when you did so and keep a copy. Do not rely on a promise to pass it on or deal with it. Busy administrators can forget.
- ✔ Oral representations should be confirmed in writing for the avoidance of doubt. This forms what is known as a 'contemporaneous record' and it usually provides the best evidence when there is a dispute about what has been said. It narrows the area about which there may be disagreement. It may prove vital in making a complaint to have such a record to show.

- ✔ Do not go to a meeting the purpose of which has not been explained to you in advance, in good time, and in writing. Ask who else will be there.
- ✔ If you are invited to a meeting to discuss your complaint always take someone with you. You have a right to be accompanied, and the university is not allowed to refuse you that right. Get the person you take to take notes, or ask to have the session tape recorded. If there are notes, send a copy of your 'record' immediately afterwards to the other persons who were present, so that they may have an opportunity to say if they believe it was not a correct record. This may be important in establishing whether the university's procedures were fair.
- ✔ If you arrive at a meeting and find that it is not as promised, leave at once, explaining why, and ask for another meeting to be arranged.
- ✔ If fresh documents, which you have not seen before, are produced at a meeting ask for an adjournment. You are entitled to time to consider them and take advice and prepare your arguments about them.
- ✔ When you present your complaint or 'case' do not make any accusations you cannot support from written or witness evidence (except in 'harassment' cases where it may be your word against the person you are complaining about).
- ✔ Be clear about the rules and regulations you have to follow in making a complaint at your university.
- ✔ Keep to the rules and regulations or your complaint may not be valid.
- ✔ Tell the truth and stick to it.
- ✔ Be consistent.
- ✔ Be persistent (universities will often stall and delay in the hope that the complainant will give up and go away).

Some thoughts for the university

The university might find it helpful to ask itself how well it could respond to the requests that a student acting on this checklist might put to it.

The institution should give some thought to its pattern of taking legal advice. It can save expenditure on legal fees to have an 'in-house' legal officer and this also has the advantage of building up experience with the types of problem that most commonly arise. Some firms work only 'for institutions' and do not take on clients in dispute with institutions. Others tend to work only for the individuals in dispute and not for the institutions. This can lead to gulfs in understanding and expectation and to difficulties about being flexible and imaginative in seeking solutions.

A university should provide all its staff with basic training in the ground rules of fairness. A university must be seen to take its decisions fairly. Training can be shown to make it less likely that disputes will escalate and become expensive and intractable.

The university should have a simple 'fairness code' that can be handed to staff and students.

A fairness code

What is fairness?

Fairness means not putting the 'weaker party', whose interests are affected by any decision (usually the student or the employee) at a disadvantage and ensuring that decisions are taken openly, on all the relevant facts, and impartially.

Different kinds of decisions are made in the university: 'academic judgements' (for example in examinations and when deciding promotions), 'disciplinary' or 'quasi-judicial' decisions, administrative decisions.

The rules that make a procedure 'fair' are not exactly the same for all kinds of decision making. It depends not only on the type of decision but also on the seriousness of the matter for the person concerned. For example, a decision leading to the expulsion of a student or the dismissal of a member of staff has to be more rigorous in the procedures that are used to reach it than an administrative decision. An appeal has to be conducted with, if anything, even greater rigour than was required in taking the decision to be challenged.

There are two main rules, known as the 'rules of natural justice', although the terminology of 'fairness' is now more usual.

The *nemo iudex* rule says that no one may be judge in his own case. This is the 'bias' rule. The same person should not act as accuser, prosecutor, judge and jury. A person who has been confided in should not take part in the decision afterwards. No one with any reason at all to prejudge the outcome should take part in the decision making.

The *audi alteram partem* rule says that both sides of the case should be heard. Under this rule come the requirements that no one should be tried in his or her absence, or without being given notice of the charge against him or her and proper time to prepare his or her defence, with a chance to question any witnesses and to see and contest the evidence brought against him or her.

Discretion

Anyone making a decision is exercising discretion. It is important to be clear how far that discretion extends, for all discretion is 'fettered' by the rules under which it is exercised. The following lists four areas that need to be addressed.

- ✔ Clarify whether the decision-maker has powers to take the decision in question at all.
- ✔ Set out under which rules the decision is to be taken.
- ✔ Draw up rules on 'rigidity' and 'exceptional circumstances'. Where rules are being followed, are they binding exactly as they stand? Where can they be varied and in which circumstances and by whom?
- ✔ Ensure that the decision-maker is not limiting his or her discretion improperly (telling him- or herself that he or she cannot do something when he or she can) or acting as though his or her discretion is wider than it is.

Further reading

Birtwhistle, T (1998) Student academic appeals: a holistic assessment, *Education and the Law*, **10**, 41–54

Bradley, A (2000) The implications of the Human Rights Act 1998 for schools, 9 June, unpublished paper

Cabinet Office (1998) *Service First: The new Charter Programme: how to deal with complaints*, Cabinet Office, London

Cambridge University (1999) *Statutes and Ordinances of the University of Cambridge*, Cambridge University Press, Cambridge

CVCP (1987) *The Data Protection Act 1984*, CVCP, London

CVCP (1994) *Notes of Guidance on Student Disciplinary Procedure*, CVCP, London

CVCP (1994) *The Higher Education Charter: Challenge and opportunity*, CVCP, London

CVCP (2000) *Independent Review of Student Appeals and Staff Disputes: Interim report of the CVCP Nolan Group*, CVCP, London

Davey, B (1992) *The Student Charter Project Report*, University of Kent, Canterbury

Evans, GR (1998) *Calling Academia to Account: Rights and responsibilities*, Society for Research into Higher Education, Buckingham

Evans, GR (2000) *Resolving Complaints and Grievances in Universities: The way forward*, Council for Academic Freedom and Academic Standards, Southampton

Farrington, D (1998) *The Law of Higher Education*, 2nd edn, Butterworths, London

Farrington, D and Mattison, F (1990) *Universities and the Law*, Conference of University Administrators Legal Group, Reading University Press, Reading

Green Paper on The Treatment of Politically Controversial Issues in Schools and Colleges [1986] PL 331

Hedley, Negligence – diagnosis of dyslexia [1999] CLJ 270
Hepple, BA, Natural justice for rusticated students [1969] CLJ 169
Hinds, W (1998) Ombudsman reports, *Education and the Law,* **10**, 81
Hyams, O (1998) *Law of Education*, Sweet & Maxwell, London
Maxwell, E (1999) Enforcement – the university as creditor, RAWS Conference, Sheffield, 24 March, unpublished
Maxwell, E (1999) The university contract, RAWS Conference, Sheffield, 24 March, unpublished
Milman, D (1986) *Educational Conflict and the Law,* Croom Helm, London
Newcastle University (1997) *Undergraduate Prospectus*, Newcastle University, Newcastle
Oxford University (1969) Hart Report: the Committee on Relations with Junior members, *Oxford University Gazette*, Supplement No.VII
Palfreyman, D (1999) The HEI-student legal relationship, with special reference to the USA experience, *Education and the Law*, **11**, 5–24
Palfreyman, D and Warner, D (1998) *Higher Education and the Law*, Open University Press, Buckingham
Quality Assurance Agency (2000) *QAA Code of Practice: Academic appeals and student complaints on academic matters*, Quality Assurance Agency, Gloucester
Report of the sit-in, February 1972, and its consequences, *Cambridge University Reporter*, **12** (14 February 1972)
Ruff, A (2000) Student Finance, in *Butterworths Education Law Manual*, eds J Gizzi and N Hancox, Butterworths, London
Smith, PM, The exclusive jurisdiction of the University Visitor [1981] 97 LQR 610 at 615
University of Essex (1974) Annan report, unpublished
University of Leeds (1996) *University of Leeds Student Charter*, University of Leeds, Leeds
Wade, HWR, Nudism and natural justice [1971] LQR 320
Weinstein, D (1979) *Bureaucratic Opposition: Challenging abuses at the workplace*, Pergamon, New York

Statutes

Data Protection Act 1998

Disability Discrimination Act 1995

Education (No 2) Act 1986

Education Reform Act 1988

Education (Student Loans) Act 1990

Education (Student Loans) Regulations 1998

Further and Higher Education Act 1992

Human Rights Act 1998

Public Interest Disclosure Act 1998

Race Relations Act 1976

Regulation of Investigatory Powers Act 2000

Sex Discrimination Act 1975

Unfair Contract Terms Act 1977

Unfair Terms in Consumer Contracts Regulations 1994, 1999

Cases

Baldry v Feintuck [1972] 2 All ER 81
Barrett v Enfield LBC [1999] 3 All ER
Blamire v South Cumbria Health Authority [1993] PIQR QI
Bolam v Friern Hospital Management Committee [1957] 2 All ER 118
Cadells v Balfour [1980] 17 R 1138
Carlton v Glasgow Caledonian University [1993] (OH) unreported
Casson v University of Aston in Birmingham [1983] 1 All ER 88
CCETSW v Edwards [1978] *The Times*, 5 May 1978
Clark v University of Lincolnshire and Humberside [2000] CA (*The Times*, 3 May 2000)
Cocks v Thanet District Council [1983] 2 AC 287
Cornelius v Banque Franco-Serbe [1942] 1 KB 29
Davis Contractors Ltd v Fareham Urban District Council [1956] AC 696
D'Mello v Loughborough College of Technology [1970] *The Times*, 17 June 1970
De Moor v Belguim [1994] 18 EHHR 372
Durayappah v Fernando [1967] 2 AC 337
D v Queen's University of Belfast [1997] ELR 431 CA
Fitzgerald v Northcote [1865] 4 F and F 656
Fowles v Bedfordshire County Council [1996] ELR 51
Freeman v Lockyer and Buckhurst Park Properties [1964] 2 QB 480
Glynn v Keele University [1971] 1 WLR 487
Gower v London Borough of Bromley [1999] *The Times*, 28 October 1999 (CA)
Herring v Templeman [1973] 3 All ER 569 at 585
Hippolyte v London Borough of Bexley [1995] PIQR 309, CA
Hollands v Canterbury County Council [1966] (unreported)
John v Rees [1969] 2 WLR 1294 at 1331
Malloch v Aberdeen Corp [1971] 1 WLR 1578
McInnes v Onslow Fane [1978] 3 All ER 211

Michael Hyde and Associates v JD Williams & Co Ltd [2000] *The Times*, 4 August 2000
Moran v University College, Salford [1993] *The Times*, 23 November 1993
Moran v University College, Salford [1994] ELR CA
M v London Guildhall University [1998] ELR 149 CA
Nagle v Fielden [1996] 2 QB 633 at 693
Oakes v Sidney Sussex College, Cambridge [1988] 1 All ER 1004
O'Reilly v Mackman [1983] 2 AC 237 at 285
Orphanos v Queen Mary College, London [1985] 2 All ER 233
Orphanos v Queen Mary College, London [1985] 2 WLR 703
Osman v UK [1998] 5 BHRC 293
Parry v Brighton Corporation [1972] 70 LGR 576
Pearce v University of Aston [1991] 2 All ER 461, CA
Phelps v Hillingdon London Borough Council [1998] 1 ELR 38
Phelps v Hillingdon London Borough Council [1999] 1 All ER 421
Philips v Bury [1692] 2 TR 346 at 358
Rajah v Royal College of Surgeons in Ireland [1994] 1 IRLM 232
Reilly v University of Glasgow [1996] ELR 394
Re Newfoundland Telephone Co and the Memorial University of Newfoundland [1984] 3 DLR (4d) 732
Roy v Kensington, Chelsea and Westminster Family Practitioners Committee [1992] 1 AC 624
R v Aston University Senate, ex parte Roffey, [1969] 2 QB 538
R v Barnet LBC, ex parte Shah [1983] 2WLR 16 at 32
R v Board of Governors of Sheffield Hallam University and others, ex parte R [1995] ELR 267
R v Civil Service Appeal Board, ex parte Cunningham [1991] 4 All ER 310 CA
R v Devon County Council, ex parte Sarah Anne Mumford CO/4463/1997
R v Her Majesty in Council, ex parte Vijayutunga [1989] 3 WLR 13
R v Hertford College, Oxford [1878] 3 QBD 693
R v Judicial Committee for the University of London, ex parte Vijayatunga [1988] 2 WLR 1106
R v Lambeth Borough Council, ex parte Walters [1993] *The Times*, 6 October 1993
R v Liverpool John Moores University, ex parte Hayes [1988] ELR 261
R v Local Commissioner for Administration, ex parte Eastleigh Borough Council [1998] 1 QB 855

R v London Borough of Bexley, ex parte Angela Bridget Jones [1994] CO 3013/93, 29 April 1994
R v London Borough of Ealing, ex parte Matharu and another, 3 May 1995
R v London County Council, ex parte Corrie [1918] 1 KB 68
R v Leeds Metropolitan University, ex parte Manders [1998] ELR 502
R v Manchester Metropolitan University, ex parte Nolan [1994] ELR 380
R v Oxford University ex parte Bolchover [1970] *The Times*, 7 October 1970
R v Port of London Authority, ex parte Kynoch Ltd [1919] 1 KB 176
R v Privy Council, ex parte Vijagatunga [1988] 1 QB 322
R v Secretary of State for Education, ex parte Standish [1993] *The Times*, 15 November 1993
R v Shropshire County Council, ex parte Jones [1997] ELR 357
R v South Bank University, ex parte Ifediora, 11 July 1995
R v Southwark London Borough Council, ex parte Udu [1995] *The Times*, 30 October 1995 CA
R v Universities Funding Council, ex parte Institute of Dental Surgery [1994] 1 All ER 651
R v University College, London, ex parte Ursula Rineker [1995] ELR 213
R v University of Aston, ex parte Roffey [1969] 2 QB 538 at 556
R v University of Cambridge, ex parte Persaud, 19 July 2000
R v University of Central England, ex parte Iqbal Sandhu [1999] ELR 121 at 134
R v University of Liverpool, ex parte Caesar-Gordon [1991] 1 QB 124
R v University of Nottingham, ex parte K [ELR] 184
R v University of Portsmouth, ex parte Lakareber [1999] ELR 135 CA
R v Visitor to the University of London, ex parte Vijatatunga [1989] 3 WLR 13
R v Visitor to the University of London, ex parte Vijatatunga [1990] 2 QB 444
R v Visitor to the University of Wales, ex parte Liam Sweeney
R v Visitors to Middle Temple, ex parte Bullock [1996] ELR 349 at 355
R v Warwickshire County Council, ex parte Collymore [1995] ELR 217 at 227
R v Warwickshire County Council, ex parte Williams [1995] ELR 326 at 333
R v West Glamorgan County Council, ex parte Gheissary [1985] *The Times*, 18 December 1985
Salek v University of Dundee [1992] *The Times*, 23 December 1992
Sammy v Birkbeck College [1964] *The Times,* 3 November 1964
Shah v London Borough of Barnet [1983] All ER 226
Smith v Nottinghamshire County Council [1981] *The Times*, 13 November 1981
Spring v Guardian Assurance [1994] IRLR 460 HL

Stringer v Minister for Housing and Local Government [1971] WLR 1, 281; [1980] 78 LGR 677
Thomson v University of London [1864] 33 LJ Ch
Thorne v University of London [1966] 2 WLR 1080
Three Rivers DC v Bank of England [1999] EuLR 211
Tuttle v University of Edinburgh [1984] SLT (OH) 172
University of Essex v Ratcliffe [1969] *The Times*, 28 November 1969
University of Nottingham v Eyert and the Pensions Ombudsman [1999] ELR 141
Van de Hurk v Netherlands [1994] 18 EHRR 481
Walker v Northumberland County Council [1995] ELR 231
Wandsworth LBC v Winder [1985] AC 461
Ward v Bradford Corporation [1971] 70 LGR 27
Weinberger and Inglis [1919] AC 606 at 631, 636, 642
Wiseman v Bourneman [1971] AC 279
X v United Kingdom [1980] 23 DR 228
X (Minors) v Bedfordshire County Council [1995] 2 AC 633

Index

Printed in Great Britain
by Amazon

36603024R00109